Falklands War Poetry

Poems written in response to the war between
Britain and Argentina in and around the
Falkland Islands, April to June 1982

Poets from Britain, the Falkland Islands
and Argentina

"Malvinas is not part of Argentina: it is part of our imagination."

Jorge Lanata, Writer, Buenos Aires

Falklands War Poetry

Poems written in response to the war between
Britain and Argentina in and around the
Falkland Islands, April to June 1982

Poets from Britain, the Falkland Islands
and Argentina

Edited by David Roberts
With assistance from Sue Littleton in Argentina

*Poems from Argentina written in Spanish translated
by Sue Littleton assisted by Daniel Ginhson*

Saxon Books

Falklands War Poetry

ISBN   978-0-9528969-5-1   Published by Saxon Books
Beaconsfield Close, Burgess Hill, West Sussex RH15 9AT UK
Website: warpoetry.co.uk
Printed and bound in great Britain by MPG Biddles Ltd, Kings Lynn, Norfolk, UK

Copyright

Acknowledgements

First, I am grateful to all the poets who have so generously shared their thoughts and experiences - often of a deeply personal nature - to convey important truths and understandings about an historical event - an event which remains, to this day, of immense importance to the people of the Falkland Islands and the peoples of Britain and Argentina.

Second I must thank Sue Littleton in Buenos Aires who, on hearing of my wish to include poetry from the Argentine viewpoint, brought tremendous energy, initiative and total commitment to the project - contacting writers across the political spectrum and including former Argentine soldiers. She not only persuaded them to write, but then translated all their work. An extraordinary achievement by Sue and the Argentine writers, completed in just a few hectic weeks.

David Roberts

Contents

Introduction - Falklands War Poetry

Falkland Islands Visit 1833

Views of the Falkland Islands - Poems

The British Experience - Poems

Contents

The Experience of Wives of Servicemen, Poems

Voices from Argentina - Poems

The Young Soldiers, The War, Other Nations Take Sides, The War in the Air, Romeo and Juliet, The Order to Sink the *General Belgrano,* Boundaries, The Survivors, What If? The Surrender, And yet . . . Galtieri's Fate, The Aftermath, Darwin Cemetery East Falklands, Peace?

Looking Back - Poems

About the Poets

Introduction

Falklands War Poetry

War poetry is not simply about real life, but it is life lived at extremes - extremes of danger, suffering, trauma, compassion, selflessness, heroism, cruelty, immorality, violence and horror. International conflicts arouse great passions, and it is clear, thirty years after the Falklands War, that feelings in Argentina are still smouldering with regard to the Falkland Islands (the Islas Malvinas) which a great many Argentines regard as Argentine territory.

The poetry in this volume springs from the experiences of the Falklands war, the ongoing psychological consequences and the continuing international dispute over the islands. It should not be looked upon as some sort of equivalent to an anthology of poetry of the First World War. Then, in the UK alone, over 2000 poets were published and they were writing about a war whose scale, destruction, suffering and duration bear no comparison with the Falklands conflict.

Views of the Falkland islands

Only one of the poems in this section by Falkland Islander, Lorena Triggs, may in any way be regarded as a war poem. *Desire the Right* expresses an absolute desire to remain free and British. In other poems she expresses a personal knowledge and affection for the landscape, climate, wildlife and a traditional event on the islands - West Falklands Sports Week. In contrast, the poems by Argentine writers about the Falkland Islands suggest that their images of the islands are grounded more in their imaginations than in reality.

The British poetry

It is hard to overstate the determination of the British government (and people) to use force to repel the unprovoked invasion of the Falkland Islands by 10,000 Argentine soldiers in April 1982. This feeling clearly ran spontaneously throughout the British services and is expressed in early poems by Bernie Bruen. His poems are wide ranging in tone and subject matter and have a rare immediacy, no doubt assisted by the fact that throughout this period he was writing daily in notebooks he kept in his combat jacket. From his poetry we learn a good deal about life under constant attack, the attitudes and philosophy of fighting men, frustrations, periods of intense activity, moments of heroism, the extraordinary work of his bomb disposal team, dealing with burned-out ships loaded with high explosives, disarming the floating mines in ice-cold water without the proper equipment for the job, and delight in surviving to see England again.

James Love gives us many vivid insights into his thoughts and experience as a paratrooper serving in the Falklands war.

Tony McNally, who joined the British Army at the age of 16, found himself at the age of 19 with huge responsibilities on his shoulders. As he sees it, he had a key role in Britain's greatest loss during the Falklands war - the bombing of the *Sir Galahad* with considerable loss of life and horrific burn injuries to many. With a colleague he manned a Rapier missile launcher. It was his task to try to shoot down low-flying jets intent on bombing British ships and army positions. As a Skyhawk jet roared in towards the *Sir Galahad* Tony McNally tried to shoot it down but the launcher malfunctioned. It refused to fire. The plane's bomb landed on the ammunition store of the *Sir Galahad* and a scene of horror blazed before his eyes.

Historians attribute the tragedy to other causes, one being the lack of naval escort, another being the slowness of the troops to disembark. Whatever the reason, the appalling scenes he witnessed and his feeling of personal responsibility have haunted him ever since.

Tony McNally's poems, like those of Graham Caldwell and Nick Lutwyche, constitute a compelling and moving account of the effects of trauma which affect some thirty percent of servicemen who have fought in battle zones. Helping sufferers with this war-induced condition is a major issue for every army. Both Tony McNally and Graham Cordwell, who has also written with great force about his personal experiences, feel that the British army has been grossly negligent in its lack of support for PTSD (Post Traumantic Stress Disorder) sufferers who, after all, had risked, and in a certain way given, their lives in its service.

Whilst Wilfred Owen, himself a victim of PTSD, wrote about PTSD as an observer, here we have the truth and sometimes shocking truths of the experience - the transformation of personality, the loss of confidence and normality, and the huge personal consequences for both the sufferers themselves and their families.

Mark Matthewson and Andrew Champion conclude this section with a tribute to a war hero, and a poem about Britain's task of returning 10,000 Argentine prisoners of war to their homeland. The British war effort was on the brink of collapse when victory was achieved. Andrew Champion, remembering looking into the faces of the defeated conscripts, remarks that he was, "staring defeat in the face which so easily could have been ours".

The experiences of wives of servicemen

The families of servicemen have always endured stress, even when their men returned home physically unharmed. Here, Louise Russell and Cesca M Croft (both pen names) write with some intensity of the unrecognised distress and heroism of long-suffering families. Although these poems are expressed in personal terms, both authors believe that all servicemen's families are to a greater or lesser degree affected and that their problems should be recognised by the armed services and assistance given. They write to be a voice for others.

Voices from Argentina

There is no tradition of writing war poetry in Argentina, although poems concerning the war were written several years later. Not one of the Argentine poets wrote about the Falklands war at the time. Nevertheless, the Falklands War was a major event in Argentine history and to the present looms large in Argentine consciousness.

When, through the internet, I discovered poet Sue Littleton living in Buenos Aires, I asked her if she had any poet friends who had written about the war. Her response and the response of Argentine poets she contacted has been phenomenal. For Sue and the other poets it has seemed as if they had been burning to write about the issue but, until now they had not allowed themselves to remember and write.

Almost all the Argentine poetry in this book was written in the space of a few weeks at the end of December 2011 and in January 2012. Two of the poets, José Luis Aparicio and Martín Raninqueo, were conscripts who fought in the war. For all the others, including Sue Littleton, the war evokes powerful memories and strong feelings. For all of the Argentine writers the war is a passionate concern.

Whilst the poets cannot be taken as a representative sample of Argentine society they do represent a variety of political opinions. A few, whilst having some regrets about the war, believe that the Falklands are inhabited by Argentines waiting to be liberated and that the Islas Malvinas are indisputably Argentine territory. Others appreciate that the islands are inhabited by people of British descent and regard the war as a shameful and foolish blunder. They consider that the Argentine government (at the start of 2012) is playing a shallow political game by once again demanding the return of the islands to Argentina.

The poems of Sue Littleton and Nina Thürler take us back into the not so distant past when Argentina was ruled by ruthless dictators. Most Argentine writers, with the exception of the former soldiers, write as detached but deeply concerned observers of the war and its consequences.

The Argentine poems have been translated by Sue Littleton with the help of Daniel Ginhson except for those by Maria Cristina Azcona and Julia Garzón-Fuentes who wrote in English.

Looking back

In the more recent poems the excitement and stress of war is absent. In its place the prevailing tone is one of thankfulness, sadness, regret and sometimes tearing heartbreak.

For our poets and all who participated in the war it was a momentous episode in their lives and for many it was life-changing.

These poems

These poems from diverse and even opposing sources tell important stories and express important opinions. This book will challenge, resonate, move, inspire, surprise or even shock - depending on the reader's sympathies with the many and varied writers. It seems only sensible that on all sides we should make efforts to understand the experiences, political and cultural differences, beliefs, problems and aspirations of others who have been or remain involved in the Falklands/Argentina/Britain conflict.

About the islands

The Falkland Islands are not the sort of place where most people would choose to live. Eight thousand miles from Britain in the South Atlantic as you head towards Antarctica are two large islands, East and West Falkland, with over 700 smaller islands scattered around, amounting to a land area half to two-thirds that of Wales. The terrain is wild, bleak, empty, virtually treeless (attempts continue to be made to introduce trees) with thousands of acres of acid peat bog. It is largely moorland without mountains, the highest hills being only about 750 metres high.

They are attractive to people who love chilly, very changeable weather, strong winds that blow for long periods, frequent light rain, vast open spaces, peace, quiet, seals, penguins, the calls of wild birds, countryside unpolluted, unspoiled by urban crowds and urban sprawl or industrialisation, surrounded by cold and turbulent seas. Temperatures are never extremely low, nor extremely high. Summer's best is 24°C. Winter's worst (mid June) is -5°C.

The British inhabitants, now numbering around 2,500, are accompanied by almost 2,000 British soldiers as a deterrent against future invasion. The language is English and the accents I have heard are like those heard in the southern counties of England. The British took over the islands in 1833. Many of the families on the islands have been there for five or six generations. Their loyalties are resolutely to Britain.

Britain's claim to the islands

With the islands situated 8000 miles from Britain and only 200 or so miles from Argentina it is natural for Argentines and the world to question why Britain should claim the islands as part of British territory.

1764 The islands were uninhabited until 1764 when the French made a settlement there.

1765-1767 A British ship visited in 1765 and raised the British flag, unaware that there were French settlers elsewhere on the islands. It sailed away again. In 1766 a British settlement was started. In 1767 the Spanish persuaded the French to leave and a Spanish governor was appointed. The French had been there for three years.

1769 In 1769 a large Spanish force from Buenos Aires arrived and ordered the British to leave after being there for three years.

1810 The Spanish colony continued until 1810 when the inhospitable nature of the islands persuaded them all to leave after a forty year occupation.

For ten years the islands were uninhabited but were visited by seal hunting and whaling ships from a number of nations.

1820 In 1820 the United Provinces of Rio de la Plata (which after much dissension later united and became Argentina) sent a frigate to claim the islands.

1823 In 1823 Buenos Aires appointed its first governor to the islands. A small settlement was established.

1832 In December 1832 Commander John James Onslow, in a ship called *Clio*, arrived at Port Egmont. He raised the British flag and ordered the garrison out. For a number of years the population remained at only a dozen or so people. Nevertheless, by the time Argentine troops invaded the islands in 1982 there had been continuous, peaceful British occupation of the islands for 150 years.

1982 - The Falklands War In April 1982 the islanders were faced with the prospect of being "liberated" by a brutal dictatorial regime from the protection of a democracy which they had freely chosen. The invaders immediately put up signs in Spanish and decreed that cars should drive on the right on the very few stretches of roads on the islands capable of taking two way traffic.

The Future of the Falklands

In recent weeks, in Buenos Aires, the British flag has been burned outside the British Embassy, there has been much chanting of anti-British slogans and calls for the "return" of the Islas Malvinas (Falkland Islands) to Argentina, and armed, masked youths, unchallenged by the police, have been throwing paint on buildings believed to belong to British companies. The Argentine government has taken steps to prevent Falkland Islands' ships docking in Argentina, Uruguay and Brazil and is making vociferous calls at the United Nations for Britain to "return" the Falkland Islands and to cease sending ships to defend the islands on the grounds that Britain is militarising the South Atlantic.

Under Article 1 of the *United Nations Charter* all member nations are committed to "respect for the principle of equal rights and self-determination of peoples."

The people of the Falkland Islands have expressed a determination to remain British and are likely to continue to do so. If they are ever to be attracted to make a closer relationship with Argentina then this is only likely to come about, in time, if Argentina offers the islanders a better economic future, trading benefits, respect for existing legal and economic arrangements, laws, and customs, reliable democratic government committed to upholding human rights, freedom of expression, and cultural diversity, educational opportunities, friendship, understanding and cooperation.

Argentina's domestic politics have moved on from violence and oppression to democracy. Argentina's government's treatment of the Falkland Islands suggests that in international relations it is forgetting the interests and wishes of the people of the islands by trying to impose itself on them by coercion. This can only harden resistance. A better relationship might be built by offering the hand of friendship.

David Roberts, 20 February 2012

Falkland Islands Visit 1833

A Report by Charles Darwin

On March 1st, 1833 . . . *The Beagle* anchored in Berkeley Sound, in East Falkland Island. This archipelago is situated in nearly the same latitude with the mouth of the Strait of Magellan; it covers a space of one hundred and twenty by sixty geographical miles, and is a little more than half the size of Ireland.

After the possession of these miserable islands had been contested by France, Spain, and England, they were left uninhabited. The government of Buenos Ayres then sold them to a private individual, but likewise used them, as old Spain had done before, for a penal settlement. England claimed her right and seized them. The Englishman who was left in charge of the flag was consequently murdered.

A British officer was next sent, unsupported by any power: and when we arrived, we found him in charge of a population, of which rather more than half were runaway rebels and murderers.

The theatre is worthy of the scenes acted on it. An undulating land, with a desolate and wretched aspect, is everywhere covered by a peaty soil and wiry grass, of one monotonous brown colour. Here and there a peak or ridge of grey quartz rock breaks through the smooth surface. Everyone has heard of the climate of these regions ; it may be compared to that which is experienced at the height of between one and two thousand feet, on the mountains of North Wales; having however less sunshine and less frost, but more wind and rain.

From *The Voyage of "The Beagle"*

Views of the Falkland Islands

Poems by Lorena Triggs, Falkland Islander, and Argentine poets Julia Garzón-Fuentes and Maria Cristina Azcona

A Sudden Snowstorm

A leaden grey hangs low where blue had just been high,
A few large snowflakes fall, then quickly multiply,
The air is still, the wind makes not the slightest sigh.

Then, like deflation of an unseen giant balloon,
The wind makes snowflakes dance to its commanding tune,
It draws a thickening blind that hides the mountains soon.

It shrieks its insults now, at every fence and line,
'Round roofs and corners too, it makes a fearful whine,
It flattens grass and bush and screams along the chine.

The wind's transparent hands play with the fallen snow,
Makes sudden swoop and toss, relentless swirl and throw,
'Tis master till it drops, to whisper soft and low.

The blue sky overhead denies a storm has been,
But earth is dressed in white, the air is crystal clean,
The sun shines now, upon a glistening winter scene.

Lorena Triggs

The Stream

Deeply within her, your mother the mountain
Bears you through caverns that man may not see,
Bringing you forth in a clear bubbling fountain,
Giving you spirit and setting you free.
Carefully over the surface you sally,

Eagerly threading each route that you find,
Gleefully tumbling towards a deep valley,
Leaving your mother the mountain behind.

Washing o'er pebbles and making them chatter,
Leaping from heights with no hint of dismay,
Into a myriad of droplets you shatter,
Locking a rainbow in fine misty spray.

As you meander, long grasses caress you,
Trout breathe the air your soul's willing to share,
Grebe, upland geese and the teal duck all bless you,
Trusting their nests and their young in your care.

'Round tiny islets you ripple and quiver,
Catching the sunlight or soft lunar glow,
Shedding your youth, you merge into a river,
Gracefully then and more stately you flow.

Rain-speckled, sun-kissed, snow-muffled you travel,
Shallow or swollen, lethargic or fast,
Seasons and years have beheld you unravel
Till salty waters embrace you at last.

Still, far away on your mother the mountain,
Ever your birth will continue to be,
Ever to rise as a clear,bubbling fountain,
Ever to race to the arms of the sea.

Lorena Triggs

Portrait of the Falklands

Islands of white sands and crashing green waves
Where porpoise and penguin hunt and play,
Whose mountains bear witness to long ago seas,
Marine fossils ever on display.

Clear bubbling springs, destined to become streams,
To eddy in pools silent and deep,

Or merrily wash over smooth pebble ways,
And tumble off falls with carefree leap.

Stone-rhymes, once fashioned by forces unknown,
Like deep scars etched in the island's side,
Where wild luscious strawberries ripen, within
The sheltered warmth these boulders provide.

Dotting the hillsides like miniature domes,
Grow balsam-bogs, each compact and neat,
The tall, hardy tussock grass bows in the wind
That carries the smells of kelp and of peat.

Unequalled scenery, course in full bloom,
Is part of the magic that beguiles,
Of the dirge of the sea to the pipes of the wind -
The melody of the Falkland Isles.

Lorena Triggs

Malvinas War

Malvinas Islands
So far away
I heard your name
Once when I was a child
Malvinas Argentinas
I was taught to sing
And still to my heart
They cling.

Malvinas war
I heard one day
Bunty my friend said
Falkland Islands
Big brother is angry.

And she was my friend
And she was English
And she was Argentine.

And the school I went to
Where I learnt to cry
When Humpty Dumpty
Sat on a wall
And all the King's horses
And all the King's men . . .
And my heart broke.

Juan López and John Ward[1]
Brave and young
Massacred and gone
Same red blood
On the icy isles
And still to my heart
They cling.

And I heard Borges[2] say
Tombs on the frozen ground
And hospitals in the snow
Better ignore
Never let anyone know
People die at war.

Julia Garzón-Fuentes

Falkland Islands

Two twins are standing there since forever.
Their beauty is a gift of the Lord.

We know that everyone
has loved them from the time
they were born.
The islands are like emeralds.
Once upon a time
in our hands they glowed.

---

[1] "Juan Lopez" and "John Ward" are names taken from a poem by Borges.

[2] Jorge Luis Borges was an important Argentine writer and poet.

We need to reconsider dialogue.
Perhaps the war has not been a solution
after all.

Perhaps it is time to send again the soldiers
to embrace each other
and try to satisfy the honour
of both sides.

Maria Cristina Azcona, 1982

West Falkland Sports Week

The Sports Week is an annual boast,
Each year a different farm is host,
The shearing done, this fun week starts,
Folk will arrive from many parts.
Some come by 'plane, a few may hike,
Still more arrive by motor bike;
On horses too, with yells and whoops,
All galloping, in merry groups.
Out yonder, on the track somewhere,
Unwholesome words disturb the air,

When 'rovers,[1] stuck fast in the peat,
Will not advance nor yet retreat.

Time passes at a hectic pace,
Whist adults, children, horses race,
With tugs-of-war to chants of " Heave!"
And trials prove skills, sheep dogs achieve;
The riders of each raging steer,
Will stimulate a hearty cheer,
They're tossed off, then it's time to run,
All adding to the devious fun.
The lively dances every night,
Continue till the dawn's first light.
"I am not tired ," someone denies,
"Just fit to drop," a voice replies.

---

[1] Landrovers

The Sports Week ends and all return
To work again, their pay to earn,
But memories of this holiday
Are certain not to fade away.

Lorena Triggs

(Written before the existence of roads.)

Desire the Right[1]

Desire the Right, Desire the Right.
This is our proud motto and by it we stand.
God keep our possession
Free from aggression.
Rest in peace, Fathers who settled this land.

Desire the Right, Desire the Right.
Friendship is offered to each peaceful stranger.
Memories are cherished
Of all those who perished.
We'll not forget those who gave us freedom from danger.

Desire the Right, Desire the Right,
Proclaimed with the passion of loyalty true.
Desire the Right.
For it, all will fight.
God bless our Queen and the red, white and blue.

Lorena Triggs

---

[1] The Falkland Islands' motto.

The British Experience

Poems by Nicholas Lutwyche, Bernie Bruen, James Love, Tony McNally, Graham Cordwell, Mark Matthewson and Andrew Champion

Musings on a small war

(Late reflections on a safe return from the Falklands War)

I watched the burials in the cemetery overlooking Ajax Bay,
grieved with their companions; thought of families far away.
There is a lonelier ground than this, so I've heard tell,
but where was it to be found? Nowhere this side of Hell.

TV and newspapers have proclaimed the fighting's glory;
for those down there it was a different tale; a truer story
of men, not all young, who fought and survived
and their unlucky comrades-at-arms who have died.

How to account for each precious life taken away –
is it enough to recall that they did their duty this day?

Tell it so to those families who, in desolation and sorrow,
have given up yesterday's light for a black tomorrow.
Tell it to men dead in the mud or floating in the sea
but for Christ's sake don't try and tell that to me.

Ships sunk; aircraft down; men missing, believed dead
good viewing on the nightly news before the nation goes to bed.
But our news was relief at another day seen through
and hope that the coming night's fears were survivable, too.

"Hit the deck, hit the deck" is the loudspeaker's awful call
as we scramble from sleep to the "Action Stations" alarm thrall.
Snapshots of one's life flash past –
grab a breath and wonder if it could be the last.

"You survived, you came home" the disbelieving voices cried.
"What of the real heroes who did not return, those who died?"
"True" my friends, "no scars to show and our faces are unlined;
but, oh, if only you could feel the wounds gaping in our minds".

"Would you fight again?" ask the silent whispers of the night,
As I try to forget the apocalyptic visions which are a blight
on my peace. Yes, oh yes, when others of my blood have lost
their freedom, their way of life; and not to count the cost.

War-broken bodies were healed, returned to a normality:
ravaged pysches festered unseen in their distorted reality.
Two hundred and fifty-five men did not return victorious from this war;
almost thirty years on, and lonely suicides have doubled that score.

Nicholas Lutwyche

Poems by Bernie Bruen
with the author's introductory notes

Bernie Bruen was commander of an eighteen man team of bomb-disposal divers in the Falklands War - Fleet Clearance Diving Team 3. The team was the most decorated unit in the Falklands' campaign. These poems and notes constitute a record and tribute to the outstanding courage and achievements of these men.

Author's introduction

From the moment of their appearance in the combat zone, the Team was in the thick of it. Immediately after *HMS Antelope* was sunk (the day the Team arrived), nine of them began the long and arduous task of removing dangerous explosives from her upper-deck and reducing the height of the wreck. This essential work continued, despite the many air-raids that were occurring, to allow freedom of manoeuvre for the rest of the landing force.

Simultaneously the second half of the Team was removing live, unexploded bombs from *RFAs Sir Galahad* and *Sir Lancelot*, thus saving those ships and returning them to vital service. After the loss of *HMS Antelope*, it had been decreed that bombs should not be defuzed but lifted out "still alive and kicking". It was these two incidents that won the Divers their bravery awards.

Fleet Clearance Diving Team 3 was based at the Red Beach Hospital where, in their spare time, they taught themselves to be nurses - a skill much in demand after the Bluff Cove incident when the casualty unit was overwhelmed with badly burned survivors.

When the Hospital was bombed, the Team was responsible for building the vast sand-bag wall between the operating theatre and the unexploded bombs to protect patients and staff from the imminent danger of explosions.

By moving their mess deck into the void space left between the blast-wall and the theatre, they not only eased the accommodation problem but also gave the Red Beach people added confidence in the efficacy of the bulwark.

The Bluff Cove incident saw a small element of Diving Team 3 as the first men to board both *Tristram* and *Galahad* (again) after the attack. Having extinguished what fires they could and checked the ships for UXBs, they then removed the stern ramp of *Tristram* with explosives to allow vital ammunition to be saved and sent to the bombarding guns around Stanley - and all this while fires raged and explosions rumbled deep in the hold of *Galahad.*

Finally, the same Element was responsible for recovering a sea-mine in a gale off Stanley, beaching it and, with minimal equipment (they had not been allowed to bring with them the specialist tools from UK), de-fusing it by hand - the first unknown, enemy mine to be rendered safe since the Korean War.

Three weeks after the surrender, the Team returned quietly to UK having suffered no casualties. Within a month, two of its members had been killed - innocent victims of other people's bad driving.

March 1982. On the way "down South" to join the Task Force, feelings about the sheer audacity and ill-mannered behaviour of the Argentinians in forcing themselves upon the population of these British islands ran high.

Thin Out!

These are our Cousins, peaceful folk.
These are their farms, their sheep, their beef.
Stand by your mettle (which I doubt).
You have no invitation - thief!
Shout if you like and yell and scream.
Send all your fighters overhead.
Strafe us with bullets, rockets, bombs;
Cripple those Ships you coveted.
Or slink and hide and run away,
Cowering behind barbed wire and mines;
Shiver and shake in quaking holes.
Hide in your scant defensive lines.
For it is ours, that earth you dig;
Possess - enjoy it for the day.
Six thousand miles we've come to state,
"The Falklands are British.
GO AWAY!"

When people began to die as a result of the inevitable confrontation, a cold determination could be found among the troops about to enter the war-zone.

We Sanctioned No Request

We sanctioned no request
From you to claim this land.
You found no warmth nor welcome here,
No friendship's open hand.

We shun that arrogance
That brought you to these shores;
You only showed aggression's greed
To steal what was not yours.

Did we invade your homes?
Did we close down your schools?
Did we dictate your way of life?
Did we impose our rules?

Or did we bolster up
Your way of life - gone mad,
And did we still regard you for
The dignity you had? - Well,

We are the British Dead
Who speak. You are accused!
By us and yours, the men you killed
And those you have abused.

We are the British Dead,
We are your slain as well.
We tend the fires that wait for you
Within the gates of Hell.

The voyage to the South was long and gave plenty of time to reflect on a previous generation, whose long struggle against similar tyrants gave their children the freedom that is so much "taken for granted" these days.

"I remembered a Sunday service in the Wellington College chapel. As the boys filed out past the Headmaster's pew, sitting next to him in the place of honour was my father, Commander Bill Bruen, the highly decorated Fleet Air Arm fighter 'ace' of the Second World War. I remembered how proud I felt and how much I hoped that I would some day be able to achieve as much."

Bequest of Honour

I wonder what our Fathers would have thought,
Could they have witnessed Sons
Trading on their Sires' heroic deeds,
With vehemence of pride,
To heighten their small standing in the School?

For though an undertaking thus discharged,
With little thought for self,
Changes one small section of the whole,
So in transition can
It cause the greater issues to unfold -

Thereafter, as the years progress in turn,
To reach along that span,
Growing weaker in its potency,
Yet able still to shape
The course of other actions by and by.

Thus did our Fathers' exploits when at War,
Indexed by the Ribbons
Proudly born, bestow upon their Heirs
Esteem and rank, conferred
By rule-subjected schoolboy parallels.

How would they think if they could but observe
Those same, if fewer, Sons
Take up Mantles laid aside in Peace
And, never doubting, stride
Away to earn authentic accolades?

Further, it was time for assessing one's place in the scheme of things and one's value to the Service. It was an opportunity to look back at what one had achieved and to wonder if, being regarded as "a bit of an odd-ball," this was perhaps the last chance to do something useful before being discarded.

Task Force

They don't want us, they want our bodies;
Need our talents, not ourselves.
Conflict calls for dedication,
Expertise enhanced by nerve.
Now ascends the banished Leader,
Outcast of promotion's cull,
Weaving spells of valour's mystic
Vital whisper, "Follow all!"

But do not bring your conscience;
Do not bring your soul.
The first you'll not be needing;
The second will be stole.

And, after years of training for such a situation as this it was time for assessing - one's own worth.

The Account

What do I have to offer my country?
My Services - they are already bought.
My Loyalty - that is understood.
Duty - Honour - were they not always there?
My Enterprise - without it I am nought.
My worldly Worth - would that I had to give.
Love of Country - that was never questioned.
No. What I have is reckoned now to be
But a gesture, an overkill; and yet
Despite the mock, the denigrating words,
I have a Life - and that I volunteer.
No man can offer more.

Sadly, not everything was as it appeared to be. Survival-suits, issued to the Team and designed to save a life in the freezing cold of South Atlantic waters, were found to be slashed, knotted and condemned - suitable only as test weights for parachute drops; and yet they had been issued as life-saving equipment.

On Issue War Stock

Slashed Survival-suits
Survived as slashed suits, not as
Suits/(slash)/ Survival;

But a slashed Suit (survival),
As a Survival-suit (slashed),
Survives suitably
To splash below parachutes.

After reaching the Islands, the Team was kept hard at work on many different and hazardous tasks which culminated in being bombed in the Hospital at Red Beach, four days later. Many of these 500-pounders failed to explode and the Team worked all night to build a huge defensive wall of wet, gravel-filled sandbags to protect the operating theatre and the wounded in the wards. At certain pre-determined times work stopped while the next notch on the bombs' time-delay-fuse ticked off - everyone taking cover. The expected explosion not being forthcoming, work resumed until once more interrupted by a possible detonation 'window'.

Hospital Blast-wall

Softly, now, and mind your noise.
Don't disturb the wounded boys - sleeping.
Though they dribble down your neck,
Put the sandbags on the deck - weeping.

Use the shingle from the shore.
Bring a couple hundred more - dripping.
Roundly, with a turn belay!
Detonator's on delay - slipping.

Time is short, so lift and haul;
Got to thicken up this wall - stacking.
"Beat the Clock to Beat the Bomb!"

Such a fitting axiom - cracking!
Strip to trousers, boots and belt.
Push yourself until you melt - sweating.
Heave 'em up; no time to lose,
Only minutes on the fuze setting.

Hacked it! - with a bag to spare,
Finest bulwark anywhere - lasting.
Let the sucker detonate;
No way it can penetrate - blasting.

Everywhere there was mud, cloying, black, peaty mud that clung to boots
and puttees with a tenacity that defied countermeasures.

Mud

As curved as an eastern slipper,
The black, glue-like San Carlos peat
Clings to the toe-cap of my boot
And overlays the camouflage
That renders me invisible.

Cracking like a blood-stiff bandage,
Each puttee, steeped in quagmire ooze,
In loosing, shows the cloth beneath
As brightly clean and livid as
The pink of newly healing wounds.

After such exciting times, in moments of night-time calm, thoughts
returned to home.

Preservation

Sink slowly into green and windswept hills,
Whose purple rocks are buttresses of truth.
Defy the cunning, soul-ensnaring ills
And leave them chase their vigil after youth.
Let passions fly, nor yet your will enfold
But join the creatures of the moors and streams.
Think their thoughts, their freedom always hold;

Make this belief the linchpin of your dreams.
Protect it in the mantle of your heart
And walk where only others' thoughts can be.
Allow your capture - so to 'come its part
And thus, in such communion, set you free.

For sailors ashore, it was sometimes difficult to know just what rank Royal Marines held.

The embroidered insignia, blended skilfully into the disruptive pattern camouflage, could only be recognised from close to, but as saluting was suspended for the duration it scarcely mattered.

Pips

Officers' badges,
Frequently indistinct on
Camouflage parkas,
Become buried by Action.
Rank holds no structure, except
To enhance the spur
Of natural Leadership.

Being based at the Hospital on Red Beach, the Divers, when not engaged in their own work, lent a hand to anyone who required it - from building sangars to digging latrine pits. They trained themselves as nurses in case they should be needed, carried in the wounded from the helicopter pads and, occasionally, those who had not survived.

At Ajax Bay

Legs lie crooked, but a fag don't help;
Bodies, shrouded with canvas tenting,
Hastily concealed, yet undisguised,
Struggle in vain for my attention.

Heavily pregnant with wounded men,
Camouflaged helos pass overhead,
Darting like birds of prey for the Pad

And the Medics of the Life Machine.
The downdraught tears the air to pieces.
Silent with the casualties' torment
Yet stunned by the engines' agonies,
It sets the ripped tarpaulin flapping.

The silver body-bags start shaking
As if their occupants, awakened
From a horrifying nightmare, were
In dread panic, thrashing to escape.

Later we shall bury them at dusk
And, on the hill, a Piper playing
The Flowers of the Forest, gravely
And with comradeship bid them farewell.

The Team suffered only one casualty. "John Boy" Walton, after diving for UXBs near the latrine outflow from the prisoners' compound, was struck down by a virulent tummy-bug.

He was, in the opinion of the surgeons, lucky to have survived. And yet he always stayed cheerful and buoyant.

Later, for his selfless attitude, along with conduct in the face of great danger that was "in the highest traditions of the Service", he was Mentioned in Dispatches.

"John Boy" Walton - Mentioned in Dispatches

They say young John Boy's
On the danger list;
He'll be lucky to survive.
How bloody stupid,
All the risks he's run,
To be killed by a microbe.
He caught it diving
On a U-X-B,
Next to the sewer.

They say young John Boy's

In the danger ward
And he's fighting for his life;
Yet, always smiling,
He hugs his trainers
To him, like a talisman.
Come on, John Boy!
You're our lucky Mascot,
You've got to pull through.

Existence in the old meat-packing plant, or the "Red and Green Life Machine," as Surgeon Commander Rick Jolly termed his Ajax Bay Hospital, was a mixture of hard work, dangerous days and long, stifling but more relaxed nights, all in very close proximity to all the other occupants.

Only the Divers had any room to move. They had set up their Messdeck (complete with hammocks) in the void-space between the sandbag wall and the operating theatre - a space designed to dissipate residual blast should any of the UXBs decide to go "bang". It became a favourite venue for parties, music, song and, sometimes, even cabaret.

At the Red and Green Life Machine

He was bathing in a pint of tepid water
And shaving in the remnants of his tea.
Coldly standing in a bucket in the passage
Was the Triage Dental Surgeon's nudity.

Sleeping soldiers packed the corridors and crossings
While Divers dumped the sandbags by the wall
Where an unexploded bomb lodged in the ceiling
And another in the 'frigeration stall.

For a hammock slung between the meat-hook girders
Can host a brief, impromptu cabaret;
But it is not easy writing home a "bluie"[1]
When the nearest light is twenty feet away.

With a pocket full of Rum and one of Whisky,

---

[1] A "bluie" was an issue letter-form that might one day reach the postman. BB.

In a cammy-jacket's mottled brown and green,
Comes the bear-like, three-ring-surgeon title-holder
Of Rick Jolly's multicoloured Life Machine.

(chorus)
Keep your head down, Mate, until this raid is over;
I would not have your job - not if you paid.
Keep your head down, Mate, until the night conceals us
Or "Warning Red" plays "Yellow's" serenade.

Then came Bluff Cove and a flood of casualties. The Divers answered the call and acted as nurses and orderlies, with special responsibility for burn victims. One was even helping the surgeons at the operating tables! All the Divers' spare clothing, what little they had, was distributed to the survivors, leaving them literally "with what they stood up in" - a distinction that would be much misunderstood later.

One young sailor from *HMS Plymouth*, which had been hit badly on the same day, grabbed the attention and admiration of the Team: although grievously hurt himself, he was greatly concerned for his "oppo," wounded in the head, next to him.

Casualties

The stretchered Sailor, by his friend
Whose hand he clasped and willed his pain to mend,
In whispers to the Medic, raised
Imploring eyes whose sparkle, morphine-glazed,
Said, "Help my Oppo, please, not me.
He's hurting bad and worse -
He cannot see."

Immediately after this, as soon as it became light, an element of the Team helicoptered to Bluff Cove to try to save *Galahad* - again - and *Tristram* too. It was a sad sight to see their old friend Sir G, abandoned and burning, a large pall of blackened smoke roiling up out of her hatchway, as explosions shook her hull beneath.

The Derelict -
RFA Sir Galahad at Bluff Cove

She lies as lies the rabbit or the doe,
With broken back and rapid, shallow breath,
Who rises even yet before its foe
And shouts defiance; shouts it unto death.

She lies and cries from pity and from shame;
Looks up to give a blind and helpless call
Whose answer echoes, calling out her name,
"No-one will come. There is no hope at all."

She lies and sighs so lonely in the dawn,
Her bulkheads at the mercy of the tide,
Her lifeboats gone, their ladders left forlorn
Who slowly swing and scratch and scratch her side.

She lies and dies; she sees the waves advance
And waits to feel them wash her life away;
Until the long, grey ships her pleas entrance
And softly come to help her on her way.

The divers jumped from the helicopter onto the still-burning *Tristram*'s deck (the pilot would not land) and set about hunting for UXBs within her. Totally dark, cold and dank, they searched with torches, their heart-beats almost audible in the unaccustomed silence. Far separated though they were, each one somehow always knew just where the other was and they emerged simultaneously on the deck - "all clear!"

Tristram at the Cove

It was all too easily definite.
All it required was to take our kit
Into a twisted Ship and climb
Ladders and walkways, a step at a time,
Down and through her cavernous bowels,
Ignoring the damage's groans and growls,
Past the engines, looming and damp,
With only the warmth of a battery lamp,

Hanging from girders blackened with soot,
Gauging the strength of the plates underfoot,
Thoroughly, doggedly, further apart,
When all you can hear is the beat of your heart,
Finding the source of the havoc to know
That nothing else lurked and was waiting to blow,
Cautiously peering in corners to see,
Silently searching - Tommo and me.

After putting out the fires and explosively removing the stern ramp to allow salvage of the desperately needed ammunition in the hold, it was time to board *Galahad* and see what could be done there. Fires still raged aboard and explosions from deep within rocked the ship. There was little that four men could achieve, beyond salvaging what gear they could. There was only one other man on board, a young soldier who had failed to escape the Argentinian attack and lay where he fell.

To a Young Galahad

Naked is no way to die, nor yet to lie
Frozen in the act of living;
At first I thought you caught in spasm,
Locked into a callisthenic dorsal arch,
Muscles - shoulder, thigh and arm -
Straining with the effort.

Then I saw your face half burned away to show
The grin of teeth that lies beneath the skin,
Your fingers burned to stubby stumps
And dog-tags gone;
Only your boots and one arm thrust
Into a shirt marked your haste to leave.

(Did you once sun yourself, running your hand
Lazily over some girlfriend's thigh
As she in turn smoothed oil upon your back?)

Somehow you died whole, unbroken
Until you tumbled to that griddle deck

That burned and scorched and seared,
Welding you to it.

Who was the man who caused your death?
Was he like those who yesterday
Pilfered through our kit, while we
Hunted bombs and rockets
Deep in a dying ship?

Your Ship is dying too, burning,
Rumbling to the explosions that
Rock the pall of blackened flames.
I cannot help her.

Excuse me if I leave you now
But there are jobs to do and fires to fight.
Snow is in the air and bleakness coming
With the winter wind.
Although you can feel nothing, yet
This tarp will keep away the chill
And clothe you for a while from prying,
Vulture eyes.

I leave you with your ship
To guard as you have done in lonely vigil;
But I will tell them where you lie
And, if tardily, someone will come
To tend you.

Back at Ajax Bay it was time to say farewell to friends and move back to one of the RFAs, *Sir Lancelot* this time. One person who loomed large in the Team's estimation was the indomitable Royal Marine Chef, Lennie Carnell, who contrived to feed them well, despite having had his first galley blown up in the bombing raid and being short on rations ("Chicken Supreme" and powdered mashed potato becoming staples). He was particularly helpful to the Divers after some of their more hazardous undertakings, putting on special meals for them at very odd times in the night. He also much appreciated the Team's Boss playing fiddle to the dinner queue to take their minds off the repetitive nature of the grub, as they threw money onto a collection plate - labelled "RNLI - support the Lifeboats - you may just need one!"

Chicken Supreme

By crossing the stonefield, into the bog,
And heading en-masse for Len's Cafe,
At dawn or at dusk, in drizzle or fog,
From vehicles, shelters, secure or unsafe,
Or the shingle-bag sangar we all improvise,
The Royals, the Matelots ask with aplomb,
"So, what have you got for us?" - Lennie replies,
"Chicken Supreme and Pom!"

Although it 'comes natural, after a while,
To crave something different - one learns;
From fiddle-tuned dinner queue - Lennie's broad smile
And passing the "oeuf a la coque" in the ferns,
For the Lifeboat will prosper, and no cause to beg,
With money they threw in the plate for that Prom
But, what was it followed the sight of the egg?
"Chicken Supreme and Pom".

A Tank Landing Craft can be fetid and cold,
Abandoned without any power;
While UXBs, shifted by chain-hoist, I'm told,
Can hold one's attention for hour after hour;
But the candle-lit quiz, when invited to dine,
Since lifting and shifting the thousand pound bomb,
"What feast can we have with that bottle of wine?"
"Chicken Supreme and Pom".

"Chicken Supreme and Pom," says he,
"A spoonful of each; that's your lot.
There ain't nothing else, apart from the tea,
But it's tasty, nutritious and hot!"

And, on leaving, it seemed appropriate to take stock of the peculiarities that the Team had experienced while guests of the indomitable Red and Green Life Machine.

Red Beach

Yes Mate, this is Falkland,
Find a sangar over there.
Bain't no demarcation.
Put your kit down anywhere.

Always keep your weapon handy
For the Argies flying low;
Air raids Red and Yellow,
Any time - you never know.

That's the Navy Divers' Castle
(called Fort Thompson); they're all mad,
Though the first to carry
In the wounded from the Pad.

There's a little extra water,
Seldom any half-way hot;
Medics take what's needed,
We can have the stuff that's not.

Them as crouching in the compound,
Argie prisoners, young and cowed,
Live on "rat-pack" Sundries
From the half that we're allowed.

That's a hole made by a bomb that
Bounced right here upon the track.
Inside two more fester,
Stopping us from moving back.

Yea! that Frigate's always waiting
Close inshore like that each day,
Since they bombed us, so's to
Keep the Argie planes away.

Oh to get there for a dhobi
Or perhaps a beer or two!
Well, it's all yours, Matey.
Keep your head down!

Aye - and you!

Came the surrender amid much rejoicing and thoughts of jobs well done; yet there waited perhaps the most hazardous one of them all - the recovery, in a gale, of a swept mine and the subsequent defusing of what was a completely unknown weapon. There was no information to go on.

The specialist tools that are required for such an undertaking had been left behind in UK: the Team had been told that they, "would not need them" and that they were, "too valuable to be taken into a war zone"!

So the job had to be done by hand with improvised tools. The chances of survival were put, at best, at 50%. The information transmitted by microwave from UK was that the device would be fitted with anti-stripping "booby-traps," put there to take out the operator.

As a Navy boxer, my feelings the night before embarking on this task were much akin to those I had prior to contesting the Navy Open final against the Commonwealth Silver Medallist, four years previously; and I felt that I should leave something of my thoughts behind, in case things went awry. No-one had done anything like this for thirty years - but then they had had the tools for it. - I did not.

Apogee

Sing no sad songs for me
If I come second in tomorrows race;
The opposition, mine to leave,
Could, with deception,
All my skill outpace.

Play no lament for me
If I misread the signals of the game;
The steadiness I must achieve
Should, with attainment,
Stay the waiting flame.

Shed no soft tears for me
If I am vanquished in the coming bout;
The uppercut I might receive
Would far surpass the
Ultimate knock-out.

In the end, after some hours of careful work, it came down to a straight choice between turning the fuse to the right or turning it to the left. One way would extract the detonator safely - the other would not - a fifty per cent chance of survival. What to do? Which way to turn?

The successful completion of this highly dangerous task marked the end of the Team's involvement in other than straight diving jobs and there was again time to reflect on life.

By now "peace" had arrived with a vengeance, along with many "Johnny-come-latelies," whose sole concession to the war zone appeared to be the fact that they did not wear ties. They had no idea who these rather scruffy divers were, with their hotchpotch uniforms, nor did they ask. However, they were voluble in their rather loud comments regarding the "cowboys", who they considered to be "letting the side down". The Divers kept their own counsel and held their tongues - but they thought, "So, you reckon that . . .

We Are the Cowboys

We are the Cowboys.
I've heard you say it loudly in the Bar,
Although well hidden by the smoke of your cigar.
We are the Cowboys
Because our hair's too long
And uniform is wrong;
We are the Cowboys
In spite of our success
And 'coz of wearing gym shoes in the Mess.

We are the Cowboys.
It must be so, 'coz Staff are never wrong.
You do not know us - but we'll jolly you along.
We are the Cowboys,
A denigrating word
To make us seem absurd;
We are the Cowboys
Because we wear no rank
And hold that certain "Johnny-Lates" are dank.
We are the Cowboys.
You think that Sailors should be awed and cowed

But we dare to be different - and that ain't allowed.
We are the Cowboys
Because we are "alive"
And that we Clearance Dive;
We are the Cowboys,
We have unique rapport
And talk with "Super-Secrets" and the Corps.

We are the Cowboys
And I suspect you'll quash us if you can;
You have the Admiral's ear. You are the "precious man".
We are the Cowboys.
You make that very clear
To anyone who'll hear.
We are the Cowboys
Because we look so "bad"
But what do you know of the jobs we've had?

Yet relationships with those "Super Secrets" (SAS and SBS) and the Royal
Marines were marked by the mutual respect enjoyed by most men of action.
When in discussion regarding the various tasks that had been allotted and
carried out, each side would invariably say, "I wouldn't have your job,
mate!"

Clearance Diver

With all the art of practised hands
And simple, fluent moves,
Deftly he turned his complicated task
To easy-actioned flow that spoke
Of skill and knowledge hard attained,
That every watcher recognised.

And all the while he chatted, talked
Of little things we knew;
Stood as an equal and with smiling poise
Responded to our questioning
Or entertained with jest and tale

That drew us ever closer still.
We looked with awe upon the man
And what he had to do.
Knowing his presence was required and why
He came at this small time and here,
We marvelled at his friendliness
And calm in the face of such a trial.

But then the time for talk was past.
He hefted up his gear,
Slipping it on his shoulders with the grace
Of long experience. The straps
He settled to their proper place
And shrugged some comfort into them.

Again with practised moves, he checked
The operation of
Levers and valves; then with a final sigh
He stopped, inert and motionless,
As in unspoken harmony
Each man became as quiet and still.

He looked at us and we at him.
His eyes behind the glass,
Calmed by the wait, had managed to retain
That sparkle that we knew; until
With sudden, almost frightening speed
That peaceful moment vaporized.

The time for action now at hand,
How flew that last routine.
Final and vital checks were carried out;
A last exchange, a muffled word,
A nod, an all embracing wave
Before he vanished from our sight.

The waters were soon smooth again,
No trace to mark his path;
Silent, we thought of what he went to face.
But which of us could ever now
Forget those special moments when
He briefly shared our coterie?

One senior "Johnny-late" was particularly patronising, speaking from a point of hearsay rather than knowledge.

The Senior Leech

Should we remark, "How right you are!"
Or with forthrightness say,
"Despite mistakes we may have made,
It was not done that way.
No doubt you will hypothesise,
Our actions to decry,
But it was us who made the grade.
It was not you - 'twas I."

We listen, dutifully bound,
As younger men must do,
While condescending patronage
Our comments honeydew.
Perhaps he's right, this pedagogue,
Pretentious, unconcerned,
But he had never seen that wreck
From which we had returned.

So, when that breeze of platitudes
Increases to a gale,
When he, unknowing of our part,
Creates some fairytale
Of our attainments, using me
As springboard to his rank,
I muse, "You swill your Brandy, pal,
But it was Rum we drank."

Suddenly came news that the Team would be on the next available aircraft for UK.

Leaving

Oh, how I long to see
The colours of England;
Green on green,

Gentled by
The wind-riven rain.
The countryside's alive there,
My spirits will revive there.
Oh, how I long to see
Her rivers once again.

The flight home was long and uncomfortable. It afforded time to put on paper thoughts about all that had been experienced, while still fresh in the mind. The Team had been to "the Edge," had looked over - and was now returning safely.

The View from the Edge

Peering from a Landing Craft stuck in the kelp,
Watching an air-raid filled with Rapier flares,
Ducking as the bullets flatten overhead;

Scrutinizing tension in a cable hoist,
Contorting, wrestling with a thousand pounder,
Waiting for the click of its fuse "going live";

Squinting at the brightness of molten metal
Showering from the bulkhead being cut away,
Wetting down the weapon to put out the flames;

Glimpsing the underside of a plane at dusk
Shrieking low over the hospital building,
Hearing its bombs detonating all around;

Seeking the route through a twisted skeleton,
Swinging above the smoulder of shipborne fires,
Hefting weighty explosives in a backpack;

Scanning bulkheads glowing in a burning Ship,
Feeling explosions stagger the hull beneath,
Covering a body - welded to the deck;

Finning backwards in a breaking wave at sea,
Fending off a Mine, a beach ball in the surf,
Recoiling from horns that one must not bend;

Reaching, later, in amongst its circuits, while
Viewing the stillness of the Falkland evening,
Musing on the Detonator, - right or left?

Here and here the limits are.
Here the unknown is revealed.

It is the View from the Edge.

Now, on the way back, similar mind-questions were asked as on
the way 'down South'. Some had been answered but yet others
remained. But over all rose the fact that the Team had taken no-
one's life, had maybe saved a few and certainly had saved ships.
None of the Divers had been injured and all had shown
themselves to be of the finest stamp of men. The questions
uppermost now were - "where to next?" - And - "would things
ever be the same again?"

The Men of the Sea

What men are these who ply the seas,
What forms of self-destruction?
What living symbols of our fate,
What victims of reduction?

What right is given them to kill,
What right for preservation?
What right to take a human life,
What price its conservation?

What knowledge do they use for good,
What knowledge use for evil?
What acts can help? What acts can harm?
What homage pays the Devil?

And when will they be free again;
And will they be contented?
And will they have the life they chose
Or will they be prevented?

And is the rocky land a curse
Or is it just depressing?
And have they left their God behind
Or do they ask his blessing?

So, is the sea their only world
Or is the land their ally?
Or do they wish to turn again
And then repent their folly?

Are they pure kindred to the sea
Or are they souls tormented?
And do they speak their mind out loud,
And is their case presented?

The answers .... they cannot be told,
The questions .... answered never.
They are the men who search the seas,
Their quest goes on for ever.

Much, much later, when awards for gallant conduct were being bestowed (when there had been time to come back to earth and carry on life as normal), the Press were there to seek out the bare bones of a story to embellish; and a different view became apparent.

Fame

Solitude's mantle,
Ripped apart by the grasping
Fingers of the mob,
Although retrieved in tatters,
Offers no sanctuary
To shroud our secrets
Nor yet our imperfections.

Courage

Viewed in battle;
Demonstrated by ribbons;
But how often shown
By the Widow answering
To the knock of a Stranger?

Four years afterwards, Bernie returned to the Falklands for a second Tour. A final task was to clear the wreck of a newly discovered Argentine aircraft that had crashed during the hostilities, and to help recover the Pilot's widely scattered bones.

Blue Ridge Pilot 1986

It is a strange feeling to take a man's hand,
In pieces, from the peat where it has lain four years,
Scraping his finger bones from the frozen ground
With a bayonet point, to stack them neatly aside.
How odd it is to find his hair still ruffled
In that rocky cranny where the cold wind explores,
And to glean scattered bones, left by the scavengers,
Seeking to catalogue his percentage presence.

The wreckage of his plane tells us how he peered
Through the blizzard, to see the ridge looming above;
How he might have cleared the scarp, but for the rock,
The outcrop that became his natural tombstone.
But rather than relate the tale, now he makes
His bed in the cold earth of Goose Green Cemetery.
Yet there is another, pleasanter feeling,
To know that at last his long vigil is over.

Bernie Bruen

Poems by James Love with notes by the author.

Fitzroy

Low and fast,
That's how they came.
Screaming low across the ground.
I swear.
If I'd tried
I could have touched it, as it passed.

A trail of death and devastation
They'd left behind.
Where the rising black plumes of smoke
Lay testament to that.

The dead, the maimed,
Trapped on a floating inferno.

In that brief moment.
Fathers, sons and brothers, died.
The lucky ones that lived.
Bleeding, burnt and scarred, shocked.

Not now, the men I once knew.

James Love says of this event, "I can still visualise the grinning SkyHawk
pilot as he passed."

May '82

May '82
It rained,
and I heard it fall.
Maybe not every drop,
but almost all.

We cut the turf.
And stacked it high.
Two foot thick
and just as wide.

Rain ran down my face
while it filled the hole.
Soaked my clothes.
Washed my soul.

No gentle pitter-patter this,
it crashed.
The wind howled, and blew.
Bayonets slashed.

And all the while,
Eight thousand miles away,
you cheered, got drunk, and slept,
in a cosy warm bed.

James Love's comment on May '82. People watched from the comfort of their living rooms. Unless you were actually there, or actually experienced war, you'll never really know.

Adrenaline

Tracer lit the night
while the screams of the dying
were drowned out
by the exploding shells.

No longer cold or wet
no thoughts of hunger.
Just a surge, a rush
the body'd come alive.

Author's comments on *Adrenaline*. It is said that war is made with long periods of boredom interspersed with frantic bursts of activity. It is.

The Survivors

You feel bad, so you have a little drink .
Another makes you feel better.
Several more make you feel great.
The devil's the barman
Hell's today, purgatory's tomorrow
Grey steel, black nights
The stars remain the same.
Eight thousand miles away,
They lie in their beds.
Dreams forgotten,
Ambitions unfulfilled.
Integrity, honour, and freedom -
Politicians' words,
For a soldier's trade is
Death.

When I Go

Place me not beneath mother earth's soil,
Dig no more trenches for me,
Entomb me not behind some brass plate,
For time to tarnish and neglect.

I still feel the cold winds of the south,
That make my body ache, yes even now.
So roast my bones quickly,
Let the flames purge my soul.

Scatter my ashes high on a hill,
Like my father before me.
Let the Scottish wind take my earthly remnants,
As I return one last time.

To the land of my birth.

James Love's comments. Use my donor's card, dispose of the packaging sensibly.

Lament for the Dead

What if I should die before the dawn?
And if I should die before the dawn,
What news ho, of me in England?
How cry you now?
Oh, men of mice!
Safe last night you slept.
It was the wind of war,
That kept me awake.
How say you now, friend?
Did we win?

That some sad price was paid
For the laughter of today
That they should not forget.
But never know
The ignominy

Of death
While in their moments of play.
Brave men died
Tho' thousands of miles away.
The same sun shone on both.

James Love

Author's comments on *Lament for the Dead*.

When I know what it means
I won't be able to post a comment.
I'll probably be dead.
Until you have had the ground beneath your feet disappear.
Seen the sky turn black and shower you with molten metal fragments,
you'll never know how precious the morning can be
for men at war.
I pray you never have to share the moment.

The Thirty Yard Dash

If he makes thirty yards
I'll get up and go.
Up and running
Jigging to and fro.

If he makes forty yards
I'll get up and go.
Is it your fear,
That seems to make him run so slow?

Go boy! Go!
If he makes another ten yards.
I'll get up and go.
Run boy, go! go! go!

Then you're there.
You're up and running.
If I make thirty yards.
Laughing as I go!

You move so slow.
If I make thirty yards.
And if I don't,
Will I ever Know?

Author's comments on *The Thirty Yard Dash*. I was that soldier. Coronation
Point, Falkland Islands, 1982. Machine gunners from hidden trenches
opened up on us.

Left a Bit and Left a Bit

Left a bit
and left a bit
and left a little more.
Now add a bit
and add a little more.
The arc's not high, as you watch it fly.
Though the chattering rattle, amidst all the battle,
causes your ears to roar.
One belt down, fifty rounds, tracer one in four.
Now left a bit
and left a bit . . .

James Love's comment. I got a hard time because I didn't have any link
for the machine guns. But I had a set of laser bino's. So spotted for them.

Forget Me Not

As you stare into the eyes
Of the man you call your friend.
To speak the words
You both know to be a lie.
You find no fear.
Maybe perhaps,
A simple resignation.
Pre-ordained. This moment.
It is Kismet.
A disciplined death.
A soldier's fate.

Author's comments on *Forget Me Not*. You take turns to draw the enemy's fire. Skill still needs help at times from "Lady Luck".

What I miss most

I miss the lads.
I miss those crisp clear nights,
when the frost glistens in the moonlight.
I miss those lonely exposed hills,
lashed by the rain.
I miss the young and innocent faces,
some of whom we'll never see again.
I miss the laughter and the crack.
I miss their morbid humour,
the childish pranks and unspoken laws.
I miss the sense of belonging,
that unique bond.
I miss youth at its best,
though I'll grow old, unlike the rest.

What I miss most ?
I miss the lads.

James Love's comments on *What I miss most*. I miss the ones that died. I also miss the guys I served in the army with. Some of them are still alive.

Poems by Tony McNally

Annabelle

How fortunate a man I am to smell
The newborn scent of my baby Annabelle
She gives me unconditional love
Her proof life must go on
Heaven-bound white dove
I pray thanks dear Lord I survived my war
In 1982 some never reached the shore

She has stopped me from taking the easy way out
That sweet smell of innocence
There is no doubt
How fortunate a man I am to tell
This is my daughter, my Annabelle.

Coming of Age

The guns fell silent, his ears ringing like church bells
Warm sunlight hit his face like a smile from God
The mist of battle drifted over his friends, no one spoke
Filling his lungs with air he could taste the cordite
Eyes stinging he thought of nothing
He was alive
He was twenty years old
A tear trickled down the side of his face
He wiped it away and pushed on up the hill.

Tony McNally's comment. After battle you are changed for ever.

Angels' Wings

Such a feeling of happiness I have never felt
Tears of pure joy so warm so loving
My Mother welcomes me, I can smell her scent
Rising up above the battlefield
My comrades smile
My enemies smile
Flying home on the wings of Angels.

Cleanse me

Wash away my hatred and black pain
Cleanse my soul of this earthly madness
Creator, if you have created, why?
Some sort of sick joke?

Death? Oh how a comfort it becomes
To love to hate to Kill
You have had your fill.
I bow at the feet of What?
It's comical even though it hurts
When all sense and reason become nothing more than an
electric spark
To ignite another bout of angst
Rain, lash these eyes that have laughed at the unfortunate,
Ridiculed the weak.
Is this my punishment?
Cleanse me, let me sleep.

Men Who Sit On Chairs

Men who sit on chairs send us to war
They tell us how to fight
They add up the score
Men who sit on chairs send us back home
Minus one or two or three or four or more
Men who sit on chairs send letters to the bereaved
They tell of the heroism of what they have achieved
Men who sit on chairs sleep soundly in their beds
Unlike the men in psycho wards being force-fed on their meds.

PTSD

I'm happy and sad
Compassionate and bad
Can't sleep at night
Can't do anything right
I wanna be alone
But not on my own
I'm in love but I hate
I'm a burden on the state
I'm possessed by the war
I killed
what for?
I see shrinks

I see docs
Remember my arctic socks
I'm disloyal cause I'm ill
Is it right to kill?
I can hide in a crowd
My face a grey shroud
I cry for no reason
My country shouts treason
All the pills and the booze
Make bad memories ooze
I was 19 in June
Under a bright crystal moon
I died that day
But I'm still here to say
For the brave and the free.
My award - PTSD.

Why do they look at me that way?

Why do they look at me that way?
"He's not all there," I've heard them say
Leave me alone you faceless folk
To fight in war it ain't no joke
I've lost my wife my job my friends
Was it all worth it? That all depends
I don't know why I feel this way
I took my oath
I did obey
I killed because I was scared to die
By blowing those Skyhawks from the sky
Those retard bombs they drove us mad
They sent us on the Galahad
The screams of the dying, twisted metal shards
A floating burning hell of dead Welsh Guards
I did not cry for them that day
Why do they look at me that way?
My brain recorded events for me
I seem to torture myself with glee
In the capital Stanley we drank ourselves sober
The Sergeant Major said "The party is over."
They sent us back to our home shore

Amongst our families we were still fighting our own war
It's nearly twenty years since we won the day
Those painful memories just won't go away
I love my Country and my brothers in arms
On November the 11th I'll sing hymns and psalms
I will wear my medals with pride on that day
The only day of the year they don't look at me that way.

Human waste

A murder of crows lands by the landfill site
I know the meaning of life
Smiling I feel slightly foolish
"What's your problem?" I giggle to a crow
Energised beyond belief
Adrenaline surge
The 9mm Browning feels cold to touch
Staring at the hand I wonder if it knows how to use it
The knuckles are hairy
White mark totally gone from the wedding finger
I'm now in love with something beyond the boundaries of this world
Don't fuck with the safety you idiot
Ha Ha Ha
Keep the weapon pointed down the range
Or inside your mouth
One of the crows looks my way
Can he see my gun?
Do crows ever commit suicide?
You're all collectively repulsive to me
I am part of the bacteria of human filth
But I'm happy truly happy for the first time in my life.

A wee dram

The young man listened in awe to the old soldier
Malt whiskey oiled the heroic deeds of the Grenadier
The same eyes that once looked for the enemy on a bloody battlefield
Now glinted from the log fires embers
Long still pauses

Deep breaths
Shaking hands
A drip of whiskey hits the carpet
Oh we were young
So very young
All dead
"Bugger Queen & Country, son"
As the Grenadier smashed the whiskey glass into the flames.

My friend the dark

"My friend the dark?"
Misty droplets of rain settle on my face like a wet mask
Slightly to the side of the grave- like trench I lie
Waiting for her to come, my friend the dark
Concentrating on the misty ground my rifle moves slightly up and down.
As my heart beats slower my breath could compromise me?
I slowly move my toes inside my boots, fear not to make the leather
creak
My guardian angel here now to watch over me
My friend the dark.
When I was but an infant the dark made me scared
Now she is my ally in this game of death
I feel a twinge in my bladder but ignore it
To die with a full bladder would it matter?
I hear a metallic click please let it be my relief
Or could it be someone else
With his friend the dark?

Violence

Heart beating magazines full adrenaline rush almost ecstatic
Not alone my brothers here, no fear no fear
Silence attacks my ears
Nervous clicking of the safety catches
Glancing to my left Smith smiles nervously thumbs up
To my left Taffy spits and wipes his brow
I'm in good company, the company of men
My mates. my pisshead nut cases
Dance Of The Flaming Arse'oles

Zulu Warriors
The Sons of Britain
Fix Bayonets
Let's fucking do 'em!

War creates Whores

My wife doesn't love me anymore
But she lied often enough
She's had a go at happy families
My she's had it rough
She has lots of family and friends
I have nobody
Love is a bad thing we all crave
I'll blame the war.
War creates whores.
Those bastard foreign shores.

Tony McNally

Poems by Graham Cordwell with his notes

Antipodean Sunset

Blood red sky, violent
Silence that grips the senses
Wind that cuts to the bone, but dries the flesh
Sudden stillness of the sunset that calms our fears

The soundtrack of our lives haunting, sometimes vivid
Clinging to a thought of a lover far away
Summer turned to winter
Antipodean stars that guide our way

Fleeting images of life and death amongst the flames
The wrenching shrills of tormented souls
A fool's overture lingers in my mind. Did his country call?
Maybe it's in my mind, not real, not false

Happy smiling faces, heavy hearts and limbs
We came so far and left so many
The elation of the moment engulfs us, intoxicating, numbing
A thought of home is shunned with painful realisation

Voices reach across the ether, time and space connect
A conspiracy of human destruction, fate is close to deal another winning hand
My mind turns to birth in the midst of death
I want to go home, but duty spurs me on

I cry inside, but no-one hears, only the guardians of my sanity
Fragile like the skin on water, one touch and my secrets overflow
Staccato glances reassure me, I'm back inside
Safe for now. Did anyone see?

Airborne Brotherhood

Whose round?
Buy us a pint?
My shout!
Lend us a fiver?

Head down
Arse up
Train hard
Fight easy

Borrowed socks
Borrowed soap
Borrowed skiddies
Borrowed time

Wotch yer back
Gotcha covered
Back me up
Won't let ya down

Gisa bit!
Gisa drag!
Gisa fag!
Two's up!

Stand still!
Stand up!
Stand to!
Stand down!

Laugh
Cry
Howl
Ache

Action Stations!
Red On!
Green On!
Go!

In the shit
Shitscared
Eating shit
Shitfaced

Strap back!
Streer away!
Say again!
Watch my strike!

Go to scoff
Go to the bank
Go to the pub
Go to sleep

Eyes right
Eyes left
Eyes front
Eyes wide

Pick me up
Take me home
Lay me down
No-one left behind

A glance
A nod

A wink
A wave

A lie
A truth
A belief
A trust

A hug
A handshake
A thought
An unshed tear

A long goodbye

Stolen Moments

Volcanic feelings, unite in love
Vows of fidelity, two as one
First cries, first steps
Wet the baby's head
Friends and brothers, all as one
Loved ones waving, inner fears

Deep breaths, pushing limits
Gritting teeth, silent prayers
Bloody corpses, sweat and tears
Sweet elation, empty souls
Laughter of a friend, gone forever
Sleep of angels, demon dreams

Leaving chaos, coming home
Hugs and kisses, repress the past
Back to normal, all is changed
Who's right, who's wrong
Silent treatment, dull the pain
Stolen moments, lifelong price

Hanging Fire

A blinding light as we pass over
Showing indifference to the selected souls
Do we have a choice?
Struggle, rage against the light
Fight the spectre, duel the scythe, find a voice
Kick and scream as you are sucked into the slipstream
We can choose to live!

Author's note: "Hangfire" is a somewhat worrying occurrence that happens from time to time, when a mortar bomb gets stuck in the barrel during firing. It is usually caused by a combination of the barrel expanding due to intense heat during high rates of fire and burned propellant residue in the barrel due to lack of cleaning.

"Hang Fire" - A pause in firing, anywhere between "commence" and "cease".

Take your pick!

Disabled

I have been labelled
What am I worth?
In a society that doesn't care
Cost-effective, best practice, clinically excellent

My "best before" date has long since passed
Arthritic joints compete with wasted muscles
Body couch-bound and clamped in situ
A life without purpose

My parameters redefined by others
Medicated, sanitised, forgotten
Held in limbo, geared down, restrained
My body a strait-jacket for my existence

Neuropathways blocked or disconnected
Chemicals surging in my blood
A juggernaut raging in my head
The outside world thundering in my ears

Drive-in, drive-thru, driven society
Without rear-view perspective
Revved up and steaming forward
No place for those who can't keep up

I am disabled by my mind
Society is disabled by my presence
I am left to ponder life
Kodak memories, filled with Prozac moments

Comfortably Numb

Running the corridor that never ends
Searching relentlessly the wall of doors
Revisited by smells and visions
Vivid as the reality that shattered into my consciousness

Dulled by alcohol and indifference
Warmed by the hearth of a strange fire
Do you know this place?

Anaesthetised, we sleep standing in our shoes
Sometimes woken by a nervous reflex
Another drink?
Sorry, time gentlemen please!

Self-medication

You embrace my soul and warm a longing heart
Fill my lonely existence with comfort on empty days
You take away my inhibitions and release the laughter behind the mask
Give meaning to my pain, my feelings find a voice

The friend in time of need, your hospitality is infamous
I cannot live without your vile caress; it gives succour to my weakness
We are a symbiosis of MADness, a mutually assured destruction
Whilst I climb the walls and plumb the depths

The grim reaper knows me well and has visited many times
Despair maintains a constant vigil

I have sacrificed my life upon your altar and loathe you with a
vengeance
But seek you out at every turn

I dare not face the day without you, even though your fire consumes me
Your demons haunt my every waking hour
I wrestle with my consciousness, a struggle I cannot win
But I will not slip this life, not yet

At last to sleep, a silent desolate refuge, a monotonous empty void
Where all thought is banished
A sublime release from all responsibility, I become as nothing
Unseen and forgotten

No angst or imposition, no pressure to perform
No feeling, nor pain
I succumb to the substance of choice, self-medicated
At least for a while

Existence

Amongst the multitude, all alone
Highly visible, but unseen
I feel, but am unfeeling
I cry, but the tears are wiped away by ignorance
I exist in my subconscious prison
Exorcised with willing precision

Author's note.
I don't mind being alone, but I hate the pain of constant loneliness.

Life on Hold – an Ode to PTSD

I do not own the causes of my pain
But they demand ownership of my mind
Grief and trauma are not contagious
But no-one wants to be touched by them
The unseen wound that never heals
The mental scars hidden from prying eyes
You pass me by with surprising regularity

Seeing what others do not
Hearing the sounds, smelling the odours
Vicious and invasive to this day
Dreaming uncomfortable visions
I cry out, remembering effortlessly and without desire
Slow-motion replays in an eternal loop
The sweat, the anguish, the shame

I should work as others to earn a daily crust
But am I valued even though I cannot provide
I once had status and responsibility, long gone
Once independent, reliable, energetic
The demons have captured me, body and soul
I stare at the flickering screen, it holds my gaze
I am overwhelmed by indecision

My mind aches for relief
Release from this mental struggle
I am tired, oh so tired of being tired
I want to sleep again without intrusion
Not to fear the laying of my head upon the pillow
Not to struggle with long nights of lonely vigil
I want to feel awake, alive, refreshed, anew

Once at the centre, now the fringe
The boundary pushing ever outward
Friends and colleagues getting fewer
The loneliness of a crowded room
Days without purpose, yet no time for thought
I see no future, but obscure the past
A haunting melody with sad refrain

I feel, therefore I must endure the moment
Attacked relentlessly by predatory thoughts
Mental knives that slash into my brain
Feelings uncontrollably surging, my heart awash with sadness
Gushing tears of bloody anguish, staunched only by chemicals
Then emptiness, a flat-lining void bereft of sensation
Empathy with the dying soul

Still here, life on hold
No rewind possible for this poor soldier

My imposed employment, to exist
Ask the existential questions, endure without respite
Fleeting moments of happiness in a sea of pain
I am a soldier still on duty, staggering on
Don't pity me, just don't look away!

Graham Cordwell

Poems by Mark Matthewson and Andrew Champion

Ode to Tumbledown

Steven Cocks introduces the poem.

While I was stationed at Ajax Bay looking after prisoners of war one of the REME Armourers took it upon himself to paint a mural. He really was very talented and as well as painting he made all sorts of bits of furniture out of old pallets. He even made some papier mâché horses and a huge dice which we used to play horse racing.

The mural consisted of a roll of honour to the dead we suffered on Tumbledown surrounded by cap badges of all the units that were with the Scots Guards that night. He borrowed mine for the Royal Army Pay Corp crest that he painted. Finally he added the following words:

Ode to Tumbledown

It was the Guardsmen of the Crown
Who scaled the Heights of Tumbledown
And fought that night a bloody fight
To see victory by dawn's first light.

From crag to crag amongst the rock,
They skirmished on, numbed by shock.
Through shell and mortar fire they moved,
Till at last the ground they'd proved

Port Stanley lay there . . . just ahead,
As they began to count their dead.
But where the glory, where the pride,
Of those eight brave men who died?

They who made that lonely sacrifice
And through each death paid the total price
In their final and heroic act,
Did surely speed the warring parties' pact.

Each one who there his life laid down,
Saved countless others from their own unknown.
So those of you who live to talk,
Let your pride hover as does the hawk.

And never let men these acts forget,
Nor the memory of our dead neglect,
But once returned across this vast sea,
Remember then just what it was to be....
A Scots Guardsman.

Mark Mathewson, 20th June 1982

Taking home the prisoners of war:

Face to face

Finally following weeks of fear and uncertainty they came
They came not to harm us but to be taken home defeated
We gaped and capered at them through the portholes
We laughed, more in relief than delight
The upturned faces smiling nervously too in relief
have haunted me since
I despised myself for it
Staring defeat in the face which could so easily have been ours
Now the survivors were going home
as we survivors would be also

And those left behind on both sides cannot smile

Andrew Champion

The Experience of Wives of Servicemen

Poems by Louise Russell and Cesca M Croft

Louise Russell introduces her poems

I am 60 years old and married to David for 40 years. David was on the *Sheffield* in the Falklands in 1982. He was reported missing when the ship was hit, then quite a few hours later it was reported that in fact he was not missing.

Since 1987 when David was medically discharged with PTSD the real David has been missing but appears from time to time which is lovely. Unfortunately, the David who came back from the Falklands refuses to leave – a bit like Jekyll and Hyde.

I believe there are many "Falklands veterans" who are also the "forgotten heroes." I mean the wives, sweethearts, mums, sisters, daughters, sons, brothers and dads of veterans. There has been a lot of writings by the vets, however, I believe it is just as important for the other side of the coin to be publicised. In almost the words of Churchill never in the field of human combat has so much been done for so many by so many who are still suffering the fallout of this conflict.

I have spoken to many families of Falklands vets and haven't come across one family who have not suffered and are still suffering because of this conflict.

I have no wish to diminish what these guys did and I couldn't begin to imagine what they have been through. I just feel that service and ex-service families' suffering is never fully realised.

PTSD is like a fungus that just keeps growing outwards affecting everyone in its path. Sometimes a little breakthrough is made to halt the growth and just when you think it's dead up it pops again.

Don't know how, but we are still together. It's only the last couple of years that my husband has become "normal".

October 2011

The Call of Home

A river of tears cannot cleanse
The unseen wound which does not heal
There are more than battlefield shells
So many human shells return home
To the family never to be the same
Children once had a dad to turn to
Now he's an island with a barrier reef
And she searches and searches in disbelief
She knows he's in there somewhere
But she cannot find the path
She doesn't know it's a one way street
It's his choice if they are ever to meet
In the land of trust where love is all around
When his spirit's journey is homeward bound
It's a long road to travel with many pitfalls
But when he stumbles her heart hears his calls
No company for him he must travel alone
But the family's love is the beacon guiding him home
Home is where the spirit longs to be
Surrounded by love then it can be free

Louise Russell

Lost

Yes you are here
But so far away
That you are not near

Your smile that never
Reaches your vacant eyes
I wonder will it ever

A heart turned to stone
Just to survive the
Pain of being alone

I don't know how
It captured your soul
Always with you now

I will find the key
To unlock your heart
And set you free

Louise Russell

Near and far

I can see your presence is here
But your spirit's in a different place
That keeps you from being near
Suspended in time and space
Where it is always that fateful day
The same scene inside your head
Will not stop it continues to play
Till your spirit is the weight of lead
Life is happening outside of your shell
Folks all around laughing and talking
Only you know that you are in hell
For you are a dead spirit still walking
And searching for the life that was
Before that trauma which seemed to halt
Your world for the Falklands' cause
The door to your heart is locked tight
Makes no difference what key you use
It never seems to fit just right
So you try to be a husband and dad
Whilst desperately searching for your world
In the land of normal before it all went bad

Louise Russell

For only just a little while

Have you ever felt so alone even in a room full of people
Have you ever felt that no one could ever possibly feel the way you do
Have you ever felt that just about everything you do is wrong
Have you ever felt your life has been turned upside down and inside out
Have you ever felt that there were no more tears left to cry
And yet still they trickle down your cheek
Have you ever felt that your whole world is spiralling downwards

Have you ever felt that your husband is so far away
When he is right next to you
Have you ever felt - why has he changed so much
Have you ever felt - why is he always shouting
Have you ever felt - why is he always drinking
Have you ever felt - why is he always angry
Have you ever felt - why does he always want to be alone
Have you ever felt - God I cannot carry this load please help me
Have you ever felt that your husband is suffering from
Post-Traumatic Stress Disorder
Have you ever felt that you would like to turn your feelings off
For only just a little while?

Louise Russell

Cesca M. Croft introduces her poem, Return from the Falklands

This poem came to mind remembering how it was, after the men came back from Atlantic duty, wondering about the attack on the Belgrano; and those who still suffer from post traumatic stress disorder - sounds of fireworks upsetting them, programmes on TV that drag it all up again, Remembrance Day services that bring the anger back. Then the medals. What were the medals for? The futility of it all.

So this is what I saw of my husband when he came back from the Falklands.

Return from the Falklands

They say that time is a healer
Time numbs the mind,
blanks out the memories.
But then you hear the fireworks
and in the dark of the night
you can still die - of fright.
Just the sound - of the bangs - all around
like guns - triggers the memory,
the fear, the cold sweats,
of being fired at -
up in the sky, over the sea,

no self defence, in foreign territory.
The crew is gripped with fear,
nerves in shreds, mouth deadly dry.
We could be dead soon.
We could plunge into the icy sea,
disappear under the Atlantic,
never to be found again.
"Lost at sea"
R.I.P.

Back home again
for a week or two.
We're at a party.
It's so unreal.
I curl up in a corner,
head in hands.
I can be me again
the real Me,
the husband, the father,
the neighbour.
This is Me.
Now I can cry.
Gentle arms hold me close.
What I have seen
won't go away.
It's still here, 20 years on,
and every firework
that you casually let off
proves that time
is not a healer.

Cesca M Croft

Voices from Argentina

José Luis Aparicio, Teresa Palazzo Conti, Juan Carlos Escalente, Luz
Etchemendigaray, Julia Garzón-Fuentes, Ange Kenny, Sue Littleton,
Alfredo María Villegas Oromí, Martín Raninqueo, Roberto Ronquietto,
Adriana Scalese, Maria Graciela Romero Sosa, Nina Thürler

Malvinas - The Return

I shut my eyes
To the scenes I saw
Of the televised
Horrors of the war.

They were young
And wounded
Their clothes torn
Their eyes blank
Their names forlorn
Their stories forsaken.

And of those who returned
Some were gone
Others killed themselves.

Julia Garzón-Fuentes

Soldiers of The Malvinas - In Memoriam

Why so many wars,
why the battles
if God has given us
the strength to speak?

Why cannot we human beings
understand
that nothing is won
by force of arms?
If we are all aware
that Christ loves us,
why create conflicts
that only bleed us?

Thirty years have passed,
and still the soul pains
for so many soldiers
who gave their lives
in the name of a cause.
We love the Malvinas,
those far-away islands:
it is not by force
that the Argentines
yearn to win them
and make them once again land of the gaucho.

British soldiers,
our prayers were with you
as well . . .
For some, for others,
for all of those
who were fighting.
And we offered masses
for those souls.

The new century has arrived,
shall we leave off arms?
Let diplomacy
say its words.
God shall bless
all the intents
of peace and calm.

The day will come
in which both nations
find a way
to escape their resentments.

Jesus is Truth,
Truth made flesh,
for this we must
believe in the Word.

Maria Graciela Romero Sosa

How Just It Is

To awaken the 2nd of April
and all the sky was Malvinas!
Our feeling was that we must help
and there was no lack of volunteers,
We women
went to our jewellery boxes
even as once the ladies of Mendoza had done
in order to help San Martín!

School children were already collecting
chocolate candy
while their mothers knitted
green caps for the soldiers.
They lived a long illusion
imagining the struggle
in the meadowlands of Goose Green
and Silent Mountain.

The months passed,
unravelling hope,
yet men of great valour and courage
came forth into the light,
the pride of millions of Argentines!

Ange Kenny

Dreams

Our dreams accompanied your preparations for war,
searching for that piece of land snatched away;
hearts united in a common cause

sheltered you.
(Blindness and ignorance.)
We did not know
that two enemies lay in wait for you
(one of iron, the other a tyrant).
The wounds still bleed
but today I can tell you
that your energy is the wing of liberty
that you made soar.

Adriana Scalese

April 2, 1982

How shall we perceive the Motherland?
What shall we do that our Motherland
shall take possession of us?
Our throats are knotted
and we are transformed into beings
worthy of our heroes.

How shall we become worthy of the flag
as it is raised
and fills with the blue of the sky
and our house with white
while fire devours our entrails?

How shall we be heroic
and forget everyday life,
know that we live for the torch
we carry inside ourselves,
the sacred fire of the Motherland?

How shall we bond together,
gaze at the aurora,
feel ourselves one people?

What shall we do that the dream of our forefathers
shall take possession of us?

What shall we do that the tatters and shreds
of which we are made

are converted into a mysterious weft
and feel the dust of our soldiers
in our fingers,
of those brave soldiers
who watered with their tears
the soil of the Islands,
our soil.

How shall we hear the voice of their destiny?
How shall we perceive the Motherland?

Luz Etchemendigaray

Thirteen Haiku by a soldier of the War of the Malvinas

The rain strikes
against the roof over the trench
(I pretend I am reading)

Cold night
(may she dream of me
lying by her side)

Nothing to be seen
except the wind
playing with an empty saucepan

Mountain sheep
from a distance resemble
flocks of clouds

Sweet is the wind
if it does not drag screams
and scatters the snow

No one in sight
except the mist
that is erasing Mt. Longdon

Fireflies of death
arriving at sunset
They come from the sea

Brusque is the wind
that pushes a soldier
wounded on the mountain

Freezing afternoon
The silence stuns
if the mortar doubts

Snowflakes on snowflakes
Red drops fall
(one after the other)

The Staked One[1]

On the peat
little green branch
dying of cold

25 de Mayo[2]

Sun on the mountain
We sing the national anthem
We pretend courage

Shrapnel

Autumn pasture
Of a rusty beast
metal scales

Martin Raninqueo

---

[1] Soldiers were sometimes staked spread-eagled to the ground as a punishment.

[2] Argentine Independence Day

Last Letter
(to my younger brother, Pablo)

There are no poplars here
nor a moon, dear Pablo.
Here there is no moon.
In the nights
there only hangs from the skyroof
(our game of deluded protection)
a portable radio
that now and then sings,
gift, last April, the great-aunt
whose name I don't recall.

I have so many silences to tell you
and, even so,
the first thing that comes to my head
is this not knowing
how I should kill
the sheep that look at me:
I aim
I load the shell
and lower the mortar barrel
while I wait impatiently
the moment to aim at the North.
But the ships are never seen.
Perhaps for this reason I angrily throw
cigars made with tea-leaves
into the air's teeth,
perhaps like gunnery fire for range adjustment
or in childish self defence.
Besides I have finally understood
that the wind
rains hangmen,
eats the stone
and causes us pain.

Now I must leave you, dear Pablo,
I will go to mark
with drool and poison
a piece of earth
that I will make mine

and in the crude instant of fear
ask of the dust
a river of savage blood in the veins
or make myself fire

beneath the wings of Calfucurá [1]
who repeated in his agony

"Do not surrender Carhué[2] to the white man,"
and then died.

But I must go out,
Juárez must be avenged,
he of the frost in his laugh
he whom yesterday a red bird
opened his forehead
in the cold centre
of his solitude.

Finally,
do not let any music box
that sounds in the world
be turned off.
This is your responsibility.
My throat, dear Pablo,
in your throat remains.

Martin Raninqueo

José Luis Aparicio introduces his poems.

I have two birth dates, one, the 15th of October 1961, and the other a little
more recent, the night of the 11th to the 12th of June, 1982. Private enlisted
in Regiment 7, friend of his friends, ex-combatant of the First Section "B",
Engineer in Constructions, occasional writer, survivor of the battle of
Monte Longdon, husband, father and proud activist of the group of the
Malvinas Veterans of La Plata, the CECIM.

---

[1] Martin is referring to his indigenous heritage. Calfucurá (which means "Blue
Stone") was a Mapuche Indian chief, who fought the Argentine colonists long
and bravely from 1832 till his death in 1873, to cling to the lands of his people.

[2] Carhué was an area belonging to the Mapuche.

In the following poems I have tried to express the sensations I personally experienced, especially the night of the battle of Monte Longdon, the 11th and the 12th of June ("Dawn" and "Not today"); waiting in the trenches at Monte Longdon ("What do you seek?"), and a rumoured possible relief of the islands ("The Relief") which finally was only that, a rumour.

Dawn is Breaking

Dawn is breaking,
slowly, as if asking for permission.
of the fog,
of the frost,
of the night.
Old night, I have
a thousand reproaches for you.

Dawn is breaking,
the darkness is casting off its mooring lines.
Other ports
are open,
other tides
await you.
The truth is I prefer that you do not return.

The cadavers
lie in the sun with their enrapt eyes,
taking form.

Old night, go away!
do not return,
stay there where you bring no pain.

José Luis Aparicio

A Relief of the Islands

Scattered by intricate paths, the trenches could barely contain our anxieties. Something new floated in the air, unprecedented, who knows by what dark magic, something that fed the desires to be once again at home.

Someone had heard that in the continent a relief of the islands was being prepared.

Naturally the news spread rapidly; sliding among the rocks it penetrated into each one of the positions, finding in each solider an amplifier, a notebook of e-mail addresses.

Toward mid-afternoon, all the First Section already spoke of the supposed relief.

I remember that I felt pierced by a sudden burst of joy and I believed, for an instant, that it was possible.

José Luis Aparicio

Not Today

Yesterday morning began rainy,
cold, windy,
irritating.
At least it began,
not like today.

Yesterday afternoon began nervous,
tense, insidious,
expectant.
At least it began,
not like today.

Yesterday night was terrifying,
cruel, without pity,
insulting.
At least it was,
not like today.

Not today.

José Luis Aparicio

Waiting in the Trenches - What Do You Seek?

Shrill whistle,
scream that bruises the air.
Metal infected with hate.
Heavy charge that seeks,
what do you seek?

Perhaps the spring where hope flows,
or maybe the velvety texture of dreams
even the weight of a tear,
or innocent love,
or you,
or me,
or your face glued to the lapel
of my quilted jacket.

Shrill whistle,
scream that bruises the air.
fatal glance of destiny.
Tense javelin that seeks.
What do you seek?

Perhaps the last bastion of happiness
or maybe all the emotion contained in an embrace,
even an unnecessary blink,
or the grinding of frightened teeth,
or the shine of your eyes
in mine,
or your smile intermittently sketched
in the water that surrounds my mattress.

Shrill whistle,
scream that bruises the air.
Inexorable presage of death.

Explosion of flesh at night.
Inwardly,
a mother
knows.

José Luis Aparicio

The Obsidian Blade of Sacrifice[1]

It is the text of terror
and there are no incantations against chaos
Fire and smoke whet the flint of sacrifice
Fate is reflected in the mirror's opacity
where children are seen with tears
of abandonment and they look face-to-face with desperation
Funerals are affirmed by agony
because in the inferior world of war there are no subtleties

In the sand pit of life
you had favourite words
What dreams what gifts what beauty or pleasure
does your heart feel in this curiosity that is death?

Details of tragedy
emerged from bastard authority
from political fiction - totalitarian action -
the adulteration of power
and useless voices of command
because there was no emancipating inspiration
It was vanity disguised as commitment
in a rallying cry for mud cold death

Mere children of a lost generation
for whom the setting was too large
in the sand pit of your games
you will no longer find a metaphor - a castle -
identity nor aesthetic lightning flashes
within the folds of your flesh
You will carry sand with every kind of asymmetry
and never again will you pronounce
the words "beauty" and "make love"
even if the obsidian blade shares
the blood of sacrifices

Juan Carlos Escalente

[1] Obsidian is a dark, glassy, volcanic rock, widely used in the Americas, before the
Spanish conquest, to make the blades of knives. It was used by the Aztecs for their daily
human sacrifice. It may be thought that young soldiers in the Falklands/Malvinas
War died under the blade of sacrifice to the gods of, perhaps, greed and war.

A Soldier of The Malvinas Known Only to God
To the memory of the soldiers who fought in the Malvinas

Today is an anniversary -
I perceive it in the steps and the voices of those
who crown the white crosses with a rosary.
Their prayers resound like a litany
beyond the cliffs
in search of those who achieved glory
in exchange for life.

I, who was born among the murmurs of the jungle
of the province of Misiones,
ask myself
how I came to these shadows
accompanied by a wind that destroys the will
and this humid earth
with its brief springs and summers
and the intensity of its colours
dancing in the surf.

Insistent,
memory returns in search of evocations
of an April engraved by fire,
furor and sorrow.

But already I have no name!
How shall I free myself after the defeat
and find the pier where luck abandoned me
to return floating over this infinity
and walk until I find the smiles of my parents
in the afternoon's return,
embody myself in the spirit of the birds
and return with my wings of freedom
to contemplate the island that imprisons me.

In the end, I did not abandon my duties.
I remained to recall the trench
where panic was transformed to bravery
and I threw myself into the senselessness of war
following the path of death.

This truth came to me in the late afternoon of that day,
when the pain of fire coursed through my body,
placed my soul in this remoteness
and closed life's path to me
that I had imagined contemplating your honey eyes.

And here I remain,
in this earth called Soledad, Solitude,
awaiting a light that foresees the end.

Roberto Ronchietto

Homage to the Naval Cruiser Belgrano

The sky was stained purple.
Like the flight of a treacherous bird
Perfidious arrow
pierced her entrails
The ocean devoured a giant
and tears of blood
wrote the dark pages of history.

Adriana Scalese

Heroes

What do they hide, these cold, solitary graves,
wrapped in the fog of oblivion?
From boy to soldier in an instant,
it was a gust of fire, madness and vain death.

Inordinate fear,
inordinate loneliness.

Rest in peace, lad.
You have not lost!

Blue and white is your sky

and although they do not say it,
you and I know
we share the bed where you lie buried.

Adriana Scalese

I The Malvinas Speak

April tore at my breathless voice
and no one could console
      my dismay.
                No one.

In this Solitude [1]
      so very mine
I am wind and storm,
peat and saltpetre among the stones
and a heartless cold that does not succeed
      in closing my wounds.

Crouched in the middle of the night
I barely glimpse the horizon
from whence the madness arises
      like a clap of thunder.

In this Southern Land
      agony burns me
to know that I was utilized by force
when they stole
      words that were mine,
putting them in the mouth of the tyrant.

There, in the North,
      a loveless iron female
nailed horror into my bones
and unleashed the dogs of war.

---

[1] *Solitude* is Soledad (in Spanish), the name of the easternmost island of the
islands of the Malvinas/Falklands. It is the only one where fighting took place.

And thus,
       stinking of gunpowder and sulphur,
they raped me in a duel of ambitions -
some,
       hungry for land not theirs;
others,
       made orphans by dying hands.

They stared at each other without looking at me.

And between them,
death incarnate in those men
who died without knowing why they were dying
and others who believed they knew the reason.

Old trenches shelter oblivion
when no one shouldered my deaths.
Only the heavy sea beating against my shores
frays itself
    in the spume's memory
    of blue and white
    flaunting a golden sun.

But truth hides itself
    among old moistures
    of sea and saltpetre
in the native land of the Yamaná Indian,
land of our fathers.

For this,
time has not succeeded in redeeming me.

A freezing wind
    caresses the peat of my belly
    where no blood
       flowers in the autumn.

II Words into the Fire

I return from the bottom of the earth
opening myself in knots tied in my blood

when the stones map the road
   that circles Darwin Hill.
A wintery wind brings to my memory
the eyes of my people
falling beyond the silences
   of the flint rocks
      of Goose Green.

Then,
  I send a prayer
cutting old flowers
   of a sea without horizons.

Other voices
   plant
   a sun
     in the storm.

I just want to see the light
as I stir my words into the fire.
April tore at my breathless voice
and no one could console
 my sorrow.
    No one.

Alfredo María Villegas Oromí

I

Autumn of 1982 at the Feet of South America

A glacial autumn has gone by
an autumn of snowstorms
of tempests and icy blizzards from the feet of America
An autumn of blood
a long autumn with young cadavers on the beach

cadavers of children

who still had in their hands
maternal tenderness
and in their eyes dawn's smile
A bewildered land watches over their skulls in the humid sand
those skulls with the perfect teeth of youthful years
and the eyes open and astonished

And the waters dyed
With hot blood
lifted their crests and covered the abysmal sockets
the violet-coloured eyelids
in an entranced gaze
and the lips bitten and closed

A drop of sea water fell in the livid circle beneath some blue eyes
and some dark eyes tried to catch the last ray of the moon
and carry it toward the sunset

The sand guards
a drop of blood
and a tear
and a drop of seawater
and the waters rise and fall
and gently spread over the slight bodies

And the evening opened the blanket of night
and unfolded its black cape over the clear foreheads
of boys who still dreamed of the games of childhood.

II

Dialogue at the Bottom of the Southern Seas

Why young friend of my own years must we meet
in this crossroads of death?

Who disposed that you and I should confront each other
leaving our sweethearts
our games
our studies
the job that we had just begun
the morning of our lives?

Who ordered that my dark eyes
should meet your blue eyes
with a sparkle of hate and scorn so alien to us?

Who decided for us that our blood
the same colour and from the same fire should mix
in the cold waters of this abyss?

My young brother
I attacked you
or you attacked me
and both of us have fallen

What history will those to blame tell?

You and I in a different meeting
in other circumstances
perhaps we could have been friends

I was not aware of the anguish in your eyes
you did not see the anguish in mine
Without knowing each other
we were enemies

But today our blue and brown eyes
sail the Ocean confused

Shall our blond and dark brown locks
braided together in a tangle
confused at the bed of these waters
serve so that someone remembers our names -

Juan and Johnny[1]
and think that there at the bottom of the seas
today we are united?

Juan and Johnny
Beneath the waters we share the same epitaph

Nina Thürler

---

[1] Juan and Johnny - a reference to the poem by Jorge Luis Borges, *Juan Lopez and John Ward* about two soldiers who were equal in death. "They might have been friends, but they saw each other face to face only once, on some overly famous islands."

Jewels

They have clear hands of fish and islets.

Like sad doves
they wind themselves together with the waters
in the nest of wind that holds them captive.

The Mother Country venerates them.

They are her distant children.

And between the white and the sky-blue
that reclaims them from on high
the soldiers walk
who do not know their name and call them "the Falklands."

With her still-wounded breast
Soledad Island draws herself together
and speaks to the Gran Malvina
of guns and blood.

She speaks to the seagulls
of the marching feet like the rolling of drums
that stuns April;
and in the scream the islands cry out
and in their strength they awaken,
and ask of men
that there be no more battles

And they entreat the men to act with enlightenment.

In the living twists of clots already dry,
the mothers, the old people,
the ploughed land, the coast,
the petrel, the schools
and the dejected veteran
they write in history:
"No more sterile clashes
no more foolish trenches
nor mourning at altars."

Teresa Palazzo Conti

Three Haiku at the End of the War

Roar, guns!
Rejoice with us
the end of the war

Blizzard and sadness
road to the Canberra
there on the high seas

Behind the fog
the boys that we were
are shouting to us: farewell

Martin Raninqueo

The Malvinas - Falklands War
A sequence of poems and commentaries by Sue Littleton

War does not determine who is right - only who is left.

"Two bald men fighting over a comb." Jorge Luis Borges, on the war of the Malvinas.

"There were many Argentines who declared they were willing to die for the Malvinas, but very few, if any, who were willing to live there." Daniel Ginhson.

The Beginning

The names lift, turn, rustle like dead leaves
in the small dust-filled whirlwind of memory
that is the not-so-distant past.
Illia, ousted president 1966 -
the generals - Onganía, Levingston, Lanusse . . .
the civilian Cámpora, - Lastiri,
and once again

Peron.
Terror sulked through the streets of Buenos Aires,
strode arrogantly
into provincial towns and small cities.
The military dragon was stoking the fires
in its great belly,
snorting and rumbling,
kneading razor claws in the hapless pelt
of the Republic of Argentina.

Many Argentines, in fear for their lives,
turned their backs on their beloved country
and fled into exile.
Most of those who fled
did not return.
Thousands of those who could not
or did not flee,
disappeared . . . forever.

The Devil's Waltz

It was the early 1970s.
General Juan Domingo Peron
waltzed back to Argentina from Spain, dipping and turning
to the dissonant music of drums and bullets.
His dull predator's eye singled out the very youth
who had adored him when they were
beyond his reach.

Unmarked Ford Falcons
were the transport of choice
and the minions of violence, machine guns
and pistols at the ready,
roamed the streets.

He was an old man by then, old and cruel and sick,
but even so he was slow in dying.
Too slow.
His uniformed body, leaking nostrils stuffed with cotton,
lay in state as the mourning crowds filed past,

wondering what was next on the agenda.
Now it was time for a murderous political two-step
and Lopez Rega, the Rasputin of the Pampas,
twirled Peron's glossy little widow Isabel
in tight circles
to the music of the Triple A Death Squad Band.

Here a Coup, There a Coup . . .

The Argentine Army, the Air Force and the Navy
were as ripe with ambitious generals and admirals
as a pear tree in the autumn
is ripe with pears.

Ciao, Isabel, adios, Lopez Rega,
the dance has ended for you.

The admirals
skipped merrily to the torture hornpipe;
and the Naval Air Force ballet leaped gracefully,
into the air,
to fling terrified partners, eyes blindfolded,
out of the planes.
Some went air-dancing drugged and stripped,
all went into the sweet-water sea
that divides Argentina and Uruguay,
and often the bodies would be washed ashore
on the Uruguayan beaches.

So the music kept on playing as the generals,
one Army, one Air Force, plus an admiral,
bounced in a high-kicking can-can.
Videla, Viola, Galtieri, the junta president-generals,
one junta after the other, pushed their predecessors
off the presidential chair
and eased themselves into power with a fanfare
of blood-filled trumpets.

And the Band Played on

They declared war on their own country,
these generals and admirals,

sporting fancy tunics hung with shiny rows
of medals and gaily coloured ribbons,
these brave military men who had never fought in any war -
perhaps convinced they were saving their country
from a leftist take-over . . . perhaps not.
Power is intoxicating.
The jails and secret military prisons vibrated in the night
with the hot jazz notes of screams
and moans and sobs

and the crackle of the *picana.*[1]

The Galtieri Junta Coup

General Galtieri and two other officers
took over the dance floor in 1981 -
from another general,
of course.

This band played wild salsa music
as the junta's chosen leader
shook the maracas.
It took only four short months
for the Argentines to realize their new president
was not only tone-deaf, but had no sense
of rhythm.

Any popularity the alcoholic President Galtieri
might have had
disappeared.
(It was common knowledge that the General
was over-fond
of expensive imported whisky.)

The Military Death Squads
continued to decimate defiant Argentine youth
who by this time had learned the score
and were involved
in their own stylish tango of bombs and kidnappings,
betrayals and assassinations.

---

[1] Electric cattle prod.

The Dirty War

Suddenly the streets were filled with enthusiastic young people
inspired by the Cuban revolution
convinced Argentina needed a new political agenda.
They chose names like "Monterneros" (Mountaineers),
ERP (Revolutionary Army of the People), Peronist Youth.
Incited by clever leaders who played on their beliefs and hopes,
they embraced acts of terrorism. Bombs,
Innocents and not-so-innocents murdered. Kidnappings.
(The ransoms paid made a few leaders very rich,
but the naive revolutionaries imagined all that money
went to support their struggle for a more equable society.)

Argentine citizens, stunned and wearied with years
of endless violence,
turned to the military to save them from this new threat.

It was rather like inviting the fox into the chicken coop
to save the chickens from the cat . . .

"War" singular was really a series
of armed aggressions against civilians.
Everything fell under the title "the Dirty War" -
armed militia against civilians, armed or not.
Men and women snatched from the streets
in broad daylight
or rousted from their beds
by thundering blows against their doors,
dragged away by uniformed men
on the whim of a general,
the caprice of some minor official,
or the sly treachery of a business rival -
to be imprisoned, tortured and summarily executed
as "leftists," "terrorists," "revolutionaries," "guerillas."

The Mothers of Plaza De Mayo

Every Thursday afternoon at four o'clock,
their heads covered with plain white scarves,
mothers of Those-Who-Had-Disappeared
marched silently
around the elegant white spire of the Piràmide de Mayo,
the monument midway in the historic Plaza de Mayo.

The repeated presence of the mothers
Wordlessly demanded information of the whereabouts
of their loved ones.
It was useless to make a formal complaint to the police
when a politically active young couple
or a son or a daughter suddenly disappeared.
If their children were dead, the mothers wanted
to know the bitter truth, have the right to the closure
of mourning.

Without this sense of finality,
the women would continue to hope against hope
their children were still alive.
incarcerated in some noisome prison cell.
It was whispered that the unborn children
of their children
were adopted like stray puppies
days after they were pushed from the wombs
of their weeping, frightened young mothers.

"Let us know! Tell us!" the voices resonate through time,
and even today
The Mothers (now the Grandmothers) wear plain white scarves
and walk the Plaza de Mayo on special occasions,
still asking questions
only the DNA of the dead
can answer.

The Pending War with Chile

Once allies in freeing themselves
from Spanish rule,
now rivals for land and one important waterway,
the Beagle Channel,

named after Darwin's famous ship.
Chile and Argentina faced off -
junta against junta.
General Pinochet glared across the Andes
at his mirror image
and General Galtieri glared back.

The superlative Argentine Air Force
stood at ready on the Chilean border,
Crack Argentine troops drilled and dallied,
waiting for a command to move out
and on to battle.

Galtieri was not comfortable contemplating
a serious war with Chile.
Pinochet did not look forward to armed warfare
with Argentina.
It was an unpopular war in both countries.
The generals already had enough on their plates
trying to control their angry, discontented citizens.

Stalemate.
Stalemate, that is, until the Malvinas, when Pinochet
could declare Chile on the side
of might and right,
supporting British forces by revealing Argentine
military and naval movements.

The Malvinas - A History Lesson from Argentina

The dispute was over the isolated archipelago off the southernmost tip of
Patagonia, consisting of two large islands and 776 scraps of wind-tortured
isles since 1833 claimed by England as the "Falklands." Over the years
since they were first discovered in the 1600's, the Malvinas had seen every
nationality come and go - French, English, Dutch, Norwegian, North
American, Spanish - traders and hunters, fishermen and whalers.

To understand why Argentines are convinced the Malvinas belong to
Argentina, a short history lesson. Originally Spain had sovereignty over
the islands, as she did over the Americas, less Portuguese Brazil. In 1764
the islands were occupied by the French and a small group of French
settlers and named the "Iles Malouines." Spain formally protested to the

French government; her protests were accepted, and the islands were returned to her in 1767. The 115 French settlers were placed under the rule of the Spanish governor at Buenos Aires.

England established a small port town on Soledad Island. Spain protested. The English withdrew and England made no further claim to the islands until 1833. In 1810 Argentina began her struggle for independence from Spain, and in 1820 the United Provinces of the Rio de la Plata, soon to become Argentina, took possession of the islands, with the approval and acceptance of Spain. There were no protests from England until 1829, when Argentine authorities prevented a piratical group of entrepreneurial English hunters and whalers from hunting seals and whales illegally on the islands and in the surrounding territorial waters of the South Atlantic.

In the final analysis, the decision by England to claim the Malvinas was based principally on commerce. Disgruntled individuals, thwarted in killing seals and harpooning whales, complained indignantly to the Crown. They removed the Spanish-speaking settlers. The islands were offered for settlement to sturdy North Scots accustomed to a cold, inhospitable climate very similar to that of the islands.

Argentine diplomatic claims for the return of the islands escalated. The settlers, given their choice by England, voted to remain British and the islands were recognized as a "self-governing Overseas British Territory." The United Kingdom accepted responsibility for defence and foreign affairs.

It's not over yet.

A Political Ploy

Galtieri needed a distraction for the citizenry,
a cause that would earn him admiration and respect. -
He had to find a way to dilute the increasing awareness
that he and his cohorts
were nothing more than vicious, blundering tyrants.
Of course! The Malvinas!
Why not belligerently insist on Argentina's
territorial right
to the virtually unprotected Malvinas?
The Malvinas were way far away from Great Britain
and the British Lion would not bother

to send the Royal Navy
halfway across the ocean on an expensive endeavour
to prevent a few sheep farmers
from becoming Argentines.
It was a masterstroke of political manipulation!
Galtieri had boldly tweaked the tail
of the startled British Lion.

Public Reactions

March 30th, thousands demonstrated
against the regime.
Tear gas and bullets. Two thousand arrested.

April 1st, people were laughing and dancing,
cheering and madly waving the national flag
in the same blood-spattered streets
of two nights before.
In the days and weeks that followed
Argentines at home and abroad
were delirious with patriotic fervour,
so caught up in the whirlwind idea of recovering
what they considered their National Heritage
they forgot everything else.

The screams of the tortured were drowned
by carefree shouts,
the echoes of gunshots were ignored
as firecrackers popped.

The Conscripts

The army netted thousand of conscripts
from the warmer provinces, trained them briefly,
and loaded them into ships
of the Armada of the Republic of Argentina.

One of those transport ships
was the *ARA General Manuel Belgrano*.

The generals quickly lowered the age of conscription
from twenty to eighteen.
Down the long, narrow length of Argentina
elated youngsters left mountain villages,
desert towns, farms, ranches, big-city streets,
dumped their textbooks, discarded their jobs
for the great adventure, the adolescent dream
of fighting a jingoistic war -
kissed their families goodbye,
and leaped, laughing and singing,
into rumbling vans
that came to bear them away.

Not all the youngsters were overjoyed at the thought
of being torn from studies and sweethearts
and sent to fight a war they didn't understand
in a distant place with a climate
cold beyond their wildest imaginings.
Some managed to escape by generous bribes
to the officials sent to recruit them . . .
The rest were not so lucky.

The Young Soldiers

It was winter,
and the Malvinas are cold, cold, cold -
scoured by chill winds and besieged by damp mists.
The youthful Argentine recruits, often the victims
of sadistic discipline,
were sent to invade that frigid land of peat and flint,
most of them from a climate near tropical
to suffer hunger and hardship
at eight degrees below zero
inadequately clothed, badly trained,
lacking arms and supplies.

The first wave of troops
captured Port Stanley,
and at home Argentines, hearing the news,
were filled with pride at the supposed victories
joyfully imagining the national flag once again
flying over the Malvinas.

Later, when the thousands of soldiers returned,
missing frostbitten fingers and toes,
disillusioned and angry,
tormented by nightmares and memories,
national pride
would give way to national shame.

The War

It was to be a hopeless, humiliating endeavor,
a "patriotic" war for political gain,
in its own way, another kind of "Dirty War,"
April 2, 1982, the Argentine invasion and occupation
of the Malvinas awakened the dozing British Lion
and an unpopular Prime Minister
with stainless steel ovaries
ordered the launching of a naval task force
to retake the islands by amphibious assault.

This time the enemy the Generals had roused
was not composed of youthful, idealistic individuals
under the leadership of corrupt men
today living fat-cat lives in Paris.

This time
the enemy was a well-armed world power.

Other Nations Take Sides

The United States made a serious attempt to mediate an end to the hostilities, Alexander Haig was negotiating a cease-fire and a truce. The British Navy, sailing toward the disputed islands, was moving so slowly it was almost standing still in the water in order to allow Haig time to convince the Argentine leaders to remove themselves from the islands.

In their joyful conviction that an air force superior in number of airplanes, manned by magnificent pilots, as well as the justification of a righteous cause, would bring them victory, exultant Argentines backed Galtieri in the rejection of the attempt at mediation. The United States, no doubt piqued by the rejection, announced it would suppress the sale of arms to Argentina and provide material support to Great Britain.

Argentina was accompanied by Peru, Venezuela, Brazil and Spain in her war. The list of nations supporting Great Britain is too long and too well-known to repeat, but neighboring Chile's dictator, General Pinochet, aligned Chile with the British.

The War in the Air

> The Fuerza Aerea Argentina, the Argentine Air Force,
> in addition to go-getting generals,
> included a group of well-trained officer pilots
> who had honed their expertise
> at military flying schools
> in the United States and Great Britain.
>
> Hampered by refuelling problems,
> the pilots flew a limited number of poorly maintained
> Douglas Skyhawks and French Mirages,
> backed by a plethora of out-of-date aircraft.

The distances from their bases prevented the Argentine pilots from using their top speed or they risked running out of fuel on the way home. Their average time on attack was only two minutes, and the A-4 Skyhawks depended on two KC-130 tankers for refuelling. In spite of these disadvantages, the FAA carried the brunt of the 74-day war and inflicted serious damage and losses to the British naval forces. Low-flying Argentine jets attacked British vessels, skimming just metres above the waves and then rising to bomb the decks of their targeted ships. The Argentine pilots showed amazing examples of courage, daring and superb flying.

Romeo and Juliet

> Sleek and deadly she was, that Skyhawk jet -
> speed and grace and beauty,
> and he loved her with a passion only pilots know
> as she thrust him across the overcast skies of winter,
> her wings hung with death.
>
> When they took off from the airfield that morning
> he was well aware of her terrible hunger and what it signified.

She could carry just enough fuel to reach
the docile, defenceless ships
cowering below her painted wings,
just enough to skim the wave tops
and slide her bombs across the decks of this one and that one
as the eyes of frightened British sailors
watched her pilot streak past, his lips stretched in a rictus.
That, and then just enough fuel
to return to base.

Exalted with his dominance of the Sky-witch whom he had
mastered,
he tempted fate that day, mocked destiny.
One pass too many, one bomb too many -
a bomb that failed to explode but played high havoc
with the ship's electrical system -
and he turned her nose toward home.
The gauges told him he had gambled
and lost.
Not enough fuel to take them to safety,
not enough to reach an altitude to fling him free of her
while she plummeted to her doom.
Desperately he guided her toward the islands
as she ripped screaming through the sky.
He coaxed and cursed and pleaded with her,
and she responded gallantly until, finally,
she could respond no more.
Together they slammed into huge lichened boulders and turf,
disintegrating into fragments
of man and metal.

They found his bones and hers entwined, enmeshed
in clinging peat, four years later.
He had been missing in action, and now,
closure.
Bits of her were left there, scattered and broken-
he lies not far from her;
a white-painted wooden cross
marks his grave.

The Order to Sink the *General Belgrano*

May 2nd. Orders were given to the commander of the elite nuclear submarine HMS *Conqueror* to attack the World War II, Argentine light cruiser, *ARA General Belgrano.*

Boundaries

The British command had drawn an ample circle
around the islands and named it
"Total Exclusion Zone."
Any Argentine aircraft or ship within the Zone
was fair game.

Unaware that the Royal Navy had decided
to change the rules, Captain Bonzo, observing
with some trepidation that his ageing ship
was being followed hungrily by the menacing shadow
of a British submarine,
hurried to push the *Belgrano* beyond the borders
of the Total Exclusion Zone,
convinced that his ship would be safe there.

The *Belgrano* was estimated to be thirty-seven miles beyond
the limits of the Exclusion Zone when she was torpedoed.
Thirty-seven miles past an imaginary line
on a ranting sea.

She was carrying 1093 conscripts, the majority age 18.
Night was falling when the ship, holed by two of three torpedoes
that slithered with deadly efficiency through that cold grey sea
was left without electric power -
which prevented her making a distress call.
The pumps couldn't function,
and the *Belgrano* began taking on water.

Two hundred were lost when the first torpedo struck.
One hundred and twenty-three young Argentines,
hardly more than boys,
drowned in the freezing grey-green waters
of the South Atlantic

or died of exposure aboard the rubber life rafts.

Nearly half of the Argentines who perished in the War of the Malvinas were on board the *ARA General Manuel Belgrano.*

The Survivors

There was no panic - the men fought the fires,
attended the wounded on deck
until the order came to abandon ship.
The *Belgrano* listed to one side
like the sad old lady she was
as the inflatable rubber life rafts filled
with fearful young men.

Night fell one hour after the sinking.
A swimmer could live only a few minutes
in the freezing waters of the South Atlantic.
The sea was heaving with mountainous thirty-foot waves
that tossed and tilted the flimsy rafts,
drenching the shivering men with icy sea water.
Winds of forty-five miles per hour added to their torment,
and many became miserably seasick
from the endless movement.

The survivors huddled together to share body warmth,
bravely succouring their wounded comrades.
Sleep meant possible death. - It was imperative
to keep the extremities moving.
Fortunately the men had eaten before the sinking,
but as the hours passed all were tormented by thirst.
There were many heroes in camaraderie
in those dreadful, interminable hours
as they waited and prayed for help.

At bleak daylight, high overhead,
planes searched for survivors.
Almost none of the men on the rafts
were familiar with the use of Bengal lights
provided to signal to rescuers . . . and anyway,
the instructions were in English.

On those rafts that carried just a few
the Argentine and Chilean rescue ships
found only the dead.
The rafts that had been crammed with men fared better,
as the men could cling to each other
for warmth.

The last raft was pulled from the water
after forty hours of exposure;
the average time in that pitiless sea
was thirty hours.

What If?

The spider of controversy spins its web endlessly.
Would Argentina have won the war
if Chile had not intervened to assist the English
whenever possible
with important intelligence information?
Were there seasoned Argentine troops
that had remained on the Chilean border, just in case -
troops that could have turned the tide at Goose Green?

What if the Belgrano had not been sunk,
and the demoralizing effect of her sinking
had not pushed Argentina to refuse further dictatorships
and to turn instead towards a democratic form of government?
What if the nation, proud of Galtieri's success in the Malvinas,
had continued to cling to her military dictators?

What if the British ships had been armed
with adequate anti-aircraft guns
and planes and pilots to attack land bases in Patagonia
or bomb the port of Buenos Aires?
What if the United States had remained neutral
and not provided radar and rockets to England?

A war, any war, arouses opinions, endless surmises.

What if.
What if, what if?

The Surrender

June 14, 1982.
The loss of life on the *Belgrano*
had torn the heart out of the Argentines.
Port Stanley was recaptured by British forces
and the Argentine military command
surrendered quietly.
The disgraceful War of the Malvinas
was over, 74 days after it had begun.

The British took 10,000 prisoners of war.
As prisoners, many of the young conscripts
were given sufficient food rations
for the first time in days.

The final estimated toll for both countries
was 900 dead -
642 Argentines, the majority conscripts,

255 British troops

    3 Falkland Islanders.

And yet . . .

And yet . . .
perhaps it was a saving defeat,
one that liberated the hearts and minds of Argentines
from their blind acceptance
of Galtieri´s Master Plan.

Argentines rebelled at last
against the many years of human rights abuses,
military coups, oppressive dictatorships.
Elections were called
and the first shaky steps were taken
on the long, difficult road back
toward justice and democracy.

Galtieri's Fate

Three days after the surrender, on June 17, 1982, Leopoldo Galtieri resigned the presidency. Reviled and jeered at by furious crowds, many of whom had demonstrated such ardent approval when war was declared, Galtieri left the government house, the Casa Rosada.

The last of the military dictator-presidents was Bignone, who remained in power just long enough to qualify him as another murdering violator of human rights. At age 85, he was sentenced in December 2011 to 25 years prison.

Nationalistic populism forgave Galtieri because he had based the war on the return of the Malvinas to Argentina. He continued to be invited to military parades and maintained his rank as a retired General.

Shortly after he was first elected president, Carlos Menem, in the interest of national reconciliation, issued a blanket amnesty for actions of the armed forces in an effort to bring closure to the highly sensitive issue of past human rights abuses.

Galtieri spent most of his remaining years living quietly and austerely until 2003, when newly elected president Nestor Kirchner revoked Menem's amnesty and placed Galtieri and a long list of generals and admirals under house arrest or in prison to await trial for the many human rights abuses they had committed.

Galtieri died at the age of seventy-six in 2003. His death thwarted those Argentines who would have had him stand trial for human rights violations with the other members of the military.

The Aftermath

Too many men had died on both sides,
but for Argentines
it was a depressing defeat in an egregious war,
difficult to discuss, painful to recall.
The humiliation of their honest pride in their country
turned against them by their leaders,
a mockery made of their patriotism and bravery,
sealed their lips, their minds, their hearts.

In the ensuing years,
belittled, mistreated, sneered at as "the crazies,"
ignored in their pleas

for recognition and recompense for their sacrifices,
as many as 354 veterans of the Malvinas War
committed suicide.
Many veterans carried the scars
of physical and psychological wounds.

Today their condition
is recognized as "Post Traumatic Stress Syndrome"
with its symptoms of altered affect, isolation,
insomnia, bleak depression.

The men were overwhelmed
by the memories that tortured them,
the physical suffering they had endured,
the friends they had seen die
in a useless, ignoble conflict.
Thousands had gone to fight as conscripts
as is established
under the Argentine Constitution,
only to be told when they later asked
for veteran's benefits
that they were not entitled,
since they had never actually fought
in a battle.

Darwin Cemetery, East Falklands

As always, some of the sad repercussions
of war (and politics) persist.
The military cemetery
where 237 Argentine soldiers are buried
lies near Darwin Settlement and the open prairie
where the Battle of Goose Green
was fought.
Tombstones are not permitted on the graves . . .
because tombstones
would insinuate permanence.

(The United Kingdom offered to return the bodies
to Argentina, but was rejected -
the fallen soldiers remain

as a continuing Argentine presence
on the islands where they died.)

Authorities do not seem to understand
that dead men make no claims to the land
where they have fallen in battle.

Plain white wooden crosses lettered in black
with the names of those known
mark the graves.
Another one hundred and twenty-three crosses
are inscribed, in Spanish,
"An Argentine soldier known unto God."

Peace?

The soldiers at Darwin Cemetery sleep on,
their war almost forgotten -
as are they.

The endless claims and complaints come and go
In the petulant tug of war between Great Britain and Argentina.
Nothing can alter the Argentine conviction that England
occupied the Malvinas by force in the early 19th century -
pulled the original Argentine settlers
from their roots and tossed them aside like unwanted weeds,
replanted the islands with hardy Scots
who prefer to remain British subjects.

The tempest whirls in the Malvinas teapot -
ships flying the Falklands flag have been banned
from the ports and waterways of the Mercosur coalition -
Argentina, Brazil, Paraguay and Uruguay.

Political history has created a Gordian knot
that international courts and sundry envoys and emissaries,
ambassadors, and attachés
break their diplomatic fingernails
attempting to untie.

British exploration companies scuttle around the Islands
insisting that a contentious dark treasure of oil has been found
beneath the stony soil
and more black gold is hinted to be lurking offshore
under that cold, cold sea.

There might have been some slight hope
for a compromise
within the next hundred years or so,
when it was still peat and saltpetre, sheep farmers and fishermen -
but oil?
Ah, now it is a different matter.
Hydrocarbons bring forth the hydra-headed dragons
of greed
and economic need.

Looking Back

Poems by James Love, Tony McNally, Graham Cordwell, Nicholas
Lutwyche, Lisa S Lutwyche, Sue Littleton, Ben Lovett, Maria Cristina
Azcona, Gus Hales, Bernie Bruen, Kevin Abbott and Lorena Triggs

One More

They'd got another one last night.
He's given up the ghost,
He'd given up the fight.
They found him early this morn.
The gaunt and haunted look upon his face. . .
The rope lay wound around the small and twisted form.
No bullet holes or shrapnel wounds,
No blood, no snot, no gore.
Just another casualty
Of a long forgotten war.

James Love

Baby's got Blue Eyes

He removed her fears,
and wiped away the tears,
as she cuddled and hung on to his neck.

The smile on her face,
matched the glow in his heart.
And he realised how lucky he was.

No one can say
there were ever a day,
when he'd never paused for thought.

The thunder rolls,
the rain lashes down,
all the while the dead lie asleep in their beds.

My turn's been.
There's some sights I've seen,
of which I'll never talk.

The breathing's shallow,
while she clutches on tight,
to her green one-eyed teddy.

He can still hear them roar,
as he closes the door,
and switches out the light.

James Love

"Season's Greetings"

The soldier sat in the packed bar all alone
Drinking his whiskey
Laughter and youthful exuberance filled the room
But could not penetrate the armour of his heart
His back against the wall giving him security
With all round defence
They never noticed him
He liked it that way
He was only there in body
His mind in a war 20 years gone
The same brown eyes staring into the nothingness
"Season's greetings" he smiled at the empty glass.

Tony McNally

Reunion

Anticipation
Will I be remembered?
A handshake
An embrace
A clearing of the throat
Swinging the lantern

The toast
Laughter at old stories heard a hundred times before
Pull up a sandbag
The rush of alcohol
Old scores laid to rest
Embarrassment, the lies, the garnished truth
The silence
A look, a nod
An understanding
Next year? Who knows!

Graham Cordwell

Author's note: My first reunion was in 2001. MV Norland's last sailing between Hull and Zeebrugge before decommisioning. As it turned out the new ship had problems, so we had to return to Hull on the Norland.

A good friend was taken ill on the voyage to Zeebrugge and placed in intensive care. He died a few months later. He was an alcoholic like me.

Eyes Left - Remembrance parade

Stiffened back, rhythmic step
Sinews stretched, muscles aching
Feet weary from a long forgotten dance

Pounding heart, proud with sadness
Moist eyes meet the marble heart of a nation
But no eyes look back

Lest WE forget

Graham Cordwell

Author's note. My first appearance as an "Old and Bold" at the Remembrance Sunday Parade at the Cenotaph in London in 2007.

Privilege

A sympathetic smile
Empathy with an underclass
An egocentric society proclaiming solidarity
Harvested from underprivileged spawning grounds
Rubbish dump kids, the defenders of privilege
Destined for unknown fields of conflict
Saviours of our democratic rights
As night follows day
Thoughts are lost in the stare of dying eyes

Graham Cordwell

Author's note. The vast majority who fill the ranks of the British Army are still recruited from working-class or underprivileged backgrounds. Many are destined to be alcoholics or homeless or even end up in prison after they leave service.

The Covenant

I played the game
I did what's right
You scratch my back, buddy buddy
The covenant, a compensation
It's many years since I paid my dues
A broken contract, a debt that's owed
Who speaks for those on borrowed time?
Existence snatched from elusive lives

Graham Cordwell

Author's note. The Military Covenant, the contract between the nation and its armed forces, has been broken for many years. Ex-servicemen and women are still having to fight for recognition, housing, employment benefit and war pensions.

Conscience

Do you see me?
I´m your neighbour, we shared a joke once
I protect your freedoms
I offend the sensibilities of a society that doesn´t care

When will you need me again?
To fight for your contrived righteousness
I´m one step away from insanity
But no-one guards my memories or inspires my future

Graham Cordwell

Author's note. I still get wound up by people who have never put their life
on the line for something, anything or even someone else, but still feel the
moral superiority to tell others what´s right or wrong.

Twenty-five Years On

Can't sleep, afraid to dream
Can't wake, too tired for lack of sleep
Can't love for fear of losing
Losing you because I can no longer love

Days turned upside down
No focus, no structure
Time disappears without recollection
I plan so much, but achieve so little

Ironclad exterior, jelly at the core
The mask is all that binds me
I struggle to mouth the truth
Do you really want to hear my story?

Crying in my dreams, transported back to '82
The gorse and peat are still burning
Lanolin, smoke and cordite
The smells offend my nostrils

Every year I´m carried back, an eternal bond
Goose Green, a brief but violent visit

Yet vivid in my thoughts
Do they think of me, as I of them?

I lost it once in '85, it only cost my marriage
A minimal price some would say, a glitch,
An aberration, that's life, it happens!
Replaced the lid and carried on

I have a life, but not worth living
Invasive thoughts of death
A simple task to end it all
A struggle to maintain control

Feelings of dysfunction
Arms and legs, diminished feeling
Pain radiating throughout a ravaged body
Saddened eyes holding back tears

I could cry, but would anyone hear me
I will not show my weakness
A sense of pride holds me tight
Duty refuses to give up

The second time was '95
I thought the end was due
But no, I found the lid once more
Renewed the armour against the world

Then, alcohol-induced psychosis
A comfortable friend
Long nights without reality
An empty, numb existence

In '02 life became a blur
A mystic fusion of realities
Raging heartbeat in my ears
Control, a seldom luxury

Struggle to maintain reality
A desire to own my fears
Fear of owning anything at all
Life without an existential meaning

If I cried, you'd see me bared
Undressed and naked as a child
I want to share my feelings
But would you survive the deluge?

I am tired, middle aged and marking time
A half-lived post war dream
Years fit snugly into thoughts
A lifetime translated into moments

Now the final bureaucratic humiliation
An intimate inquisition, irrefutable proof of life
Ill and tired of repetition, I want to rest,
To be finished, 25 years on

Graham Cordwell

The Abandoned Soldier

The eyes betray the pain
Hollow, empty eyes
A lifetime in one glance
Blinking moist with sadness
In search of understanding
Barely holding back the tear

Alone, standing to attention
A solemn sight for all to view
A stubborn look about the face
Lips taut with embers of defiance
A wry ironic smile
A stoic sense of duty

The glorious dead do not grow old
The living are but vague reminders
Of a soldier's gift and a nation's debt
A collective shame unwashed in generations
Putrid and bitter without a voice
Crying out for respect and restitution

Body racked with untold hurt
Phantom pain from near-useless limbs

Age has wearied him
And the years condemned
The shadow of a once proud man
Who took the shilling and paid the price

Young men, old beyond their years
Damaged minds in ravaged bodies
Witness to the horrors
Victim of the daily struggle
Stiffened with age and unseen scars
He does not complain, we taught him well

Communities of dead from conflicts past
Stand testament to our human failure
Leaders give no deference to the fallen
Dulce et decorum est . . . the oldest lie,
Loved ones nurse a heavy burden
Complicit in their fervour

Hand picked like poppies of the field
Blossoms of the poor and disadvantaged
Moulded to be the nation,s guardians
Hailed as saviours in the morning
Old heroes slowly fade away
Discarded when the sun goes down

In the autumn of our lives
Old soldiers reminisce
Amidst the dreams of death and glory
Two minutes can seem a lifetime
In remembrance of the fallen
A fleeting memory remiss

The promise has been broken
No longer duty-bound
Honour lies bloody on the altar
A sacrificial lamb
The soldier has been abandoned
In a society that doesn't care

Graham Cordwell

PTSD

Decades later, there are days when it is forgotten,
until some flickering image or incoherent sound
commands an unwanted replay of the old news,
recreating those images of family flashing past
preceding playback of combat that destroys my peace.

Then, violent shadows of lonely death haunt me.
The winged missiles that seek out ships,
bring the rage of fire, flood and smoke -
backdrop for the cries of wounded men,
and the quiet of sudden death.

The silvery screening of those tiny airplanes, searching
for my ship, my fellow seafarers, transfixes me.
Sweat glistens, body hair stands up, I'm holding my breath.
Honey, she says, leaning across the settee,
Come back, talk to me – please.
So many years on,
and my silent, lost comrades will not let me speak.

Nicholas Lutwyche

Relativity

It looks old, suddenly,
slack-skinned and veins raised -
the back of his hand
which rests on the sleek fur
of the sleeping cat.

She purrs, curled upon his legs,
the surety of youth runs in her veins,
blue eyes not clouded by cataracts;
while he sits in the silver, flickering light.

He will have to put her away
one day, and lose another friend;
grieve for her companionship
after her nine short lives disappear,
speeding past his reluctant years.

It is all so temporary, this life.
Grief, happiness, pain and delight
drift through our senses as
autumn mists mingling with
turning leaves on tall trees.

Folded carefully on military coffins
other colors reflect a different fall.
The old hand trembles in a last salute
and returns gently to rest with the cat;
feline peace calming an uneasy mind.

Nicholas Lutwyche

Fallen

It seems as though there are more leaves
than I remember gathering a year ago.
Perhaps the old rake has shrunk in the rain
or memory, more often of late, has faltered.

Each new Autumnal crop spreads further
and my aching back feels weaker.

To live in the serenity of trees
requires, after all, some sacrifice
but not as great as that made by those
whose war-graves lie among these leaves

Nicholas Lutwyche

Will You Remember?

The final reunion will be here
soon enough;
all those long tables set
with candelabra and gleaming plates.
The chairs empty; silent and untended.

No more cold Remembrance Day parades
in grey November rain, with

mournful bugles calling across lowered flags
for those now beyond the common sight…

beyond the heart-clenching reach
Of "Action Stations" alarms;
the sea ghosts have slipped their anchor chains,
dissolving down channel
into the mists of final peace.

Discarded lie the paraphernalia of war,
the rituals; the anniversaries afterwards
dwindle into obscurity and neglect
with the passing of the last, lonely souls.

Nicholas Lutwyche

Deconstruction

(In 2011 HMS Invincible, icon of the Falklands War, was towed
from Portsmouth Naval Dockyard for scrap.)

In our house is a painting of the ship that battled
crashing oceans and floated my husband to his War.
Tiny men line the decks at attention, in full dress,
ready for the welcome of Queen and Country.
My husband is one of them.

In the painting the great ship is greeted
with all the fanfare a victorious warrior deserves.
Rust streams down her hull like blood from wounds.
I can hear military bands and the cheers of crowds.
Though I didn't know him yet.

In England we gathered in our finest clothes.
We attended a sombre ceremony that relieved her of her duty.
That dusk the bugle stirred even my civilian heart.
British men struggled for composure, another battle
to withstand, but we women wept.

A knighted admiral, the man who brought them
"there and back" squared his shoulders, stiff and poised.

What surged through him as he saluted his men
and his most significant, beloved ship
that final time?

Today my husband shows me a photograph.
The proud ship, her shapely hull still discernible,
stands mute, in a shipyard, surrounded by cranes.
It looks like her assembly, but it is her undoing, her dismantling,
her deconstruction.

I know where his berth was, now exposed.
There are the corridors that haunt his dreams,
where alarms sounded, danger was announced, and death waited.
They gape now, emptied arteries,
open to the sea.

We have an understanding, his ship and his wife.
Displayed in our American home, I pass her every day.
I know they are locked in an unending embrace.
She is his beloved and his nemesis, sometimes an unwitting
partner to another deconstruction. His.

Lisa S Lutwyche

Seeds of War

Today, on Soledad Island,
the same chill wind that blows ceaselessly
across the graves in Darwin Cemetery
scuds and twines around the hooded, dark-faced men
who walk the empty fields near Sapper's Hill
and the beaches huddled behind barbed wire fences.
The area is staked with bright red signs marked
with a neat white skull and crossbones
and the warning "Danger!"

The Argentine military, after taking Port Stanley,
were convinced English forces would invade Soledad
so they buried antipersonnel mines
in 113 different areas,
assuring that those locales would remain indefinitely

off-limits to man and beast.
The islanders have posted discreet notices in public buildings
that mention that the Argentines
left behind over 25,000 explosive surprises.
Argentines claim they only planted 15,000 mines
to enliven picnics in the open.
Tourists, please don't wander past those barbed wire fences
marked with warning signs.
Herders, keep your distance and the same goes
for your sheep (fortunately, the only victims so far).

The expert sappers, originally from tropical Zimbabwe,
have come with their yellow-painted divining rods
attached to a box that buzzes
like a thousand angry bees when the rod finds metal.
It is estimated that it will take thirty years
to remove all the mines...
In the meantime, the handful of black-uniformed men
shiver in the mist that rises when the wind dies a little.
They remember searching other minefields in other countries,
abandoned regions harboring the cruel debris
that for years will promise mutilation and death
to the unwary innocent.

Sue Littleton
9 February 2012

My Father

Ben Lovett introduces the poem he wrote as a boy.

My Father, Christopher Lovett, was a medic with the Third Battalion
Parachute Regiment and was killed in action on the morning of the 12th
June on Mount Longdon, while treating the injured. I was only 2 and a
half at the time.
I went to the Falklands in 1991 when I was about ten years-old or so.
Upon my return, back at boarding school in Christ's Hospital near
Horsham, in the UK, I wrote this poem, and to this day, I still remember
it.

- 1 February 2012

My Father

My Father wore a red beret
He wore it with great pride

One day he went,
leaving Mother by my side

They fought a mighty battle
For some the fight was brief

So I honour him and others too
Who lay here by his side

They say time heals many things
It really isn't true

For I have loved and missed you, Dad
It seems my whole life through

Ben Lovett

Malvinas

Peace far and beyond
Under blue and green waves of sorrow
Hundreds of soldiers have died and are gone
We need to survive under their shadowy night

Malvinas are Argentinian islands
They are ours, you must understand this now
Don't you see we don't want them for money or oil
Simply we love them as they are our daughters

Peace far and beyond the sorrowful night
Soldiers cry, their feet bleeding in coldness
Twenty years old, the survivors committed suicide
Three hundred have decided to share the sorrowful night

They are gone too far
The war is not ending yet
three hundred children are gone
They joined the victims of the war

Maria Cristina Azcona
Argentina

Victory

Every year on Remembrance Sunday
I sit in the corner of the British Legion bar
Dressed in blazer, shirt, regimental tie, polished shoes,
With my head held high.
But deep in my mind where nobody goes
I see a wooden cross where the wind of victory blows.
"Three cheers for victory," I heard the politicians say
But they never asked me about my victory.
If they had, I would have explained it this way.
It isn't your flags or your emblems of war
Or your marching of troops past the palace's door.
It isn't Mrs Thatcher on the balcony high
Reaffirming her pledge to serve or to die.
But it's the look, and the pain on the teenager's face
As he dies for his country in a far off place.
It's the guns, and the shells and phosphorous grenades,
The dead and wounded, the freshly cut graves
Or a grieving wife with a fatherless child
Whose young tender life will be forever deprived,
Or the alcoholic soldier with a shattered mind
Who takes the suicide option for some peace to find.
Well that's my victory but no one knows.
It's deep in my mind where nobody goes.

Gus Hales

This poem was spoken by Gus at the Remembrance Day Service at Christ
Church Cathedral, Stanley, Falkland Islands, 11 November 2007.

Bernie Bruen introduces *To a Young Galahad - Thirty Years on*

Last week I was in Stamford being filmed for a documentary for Channel 5, a British TV station. It was about the bomb disposal effort we put in during the Falklands war. All was going smoothly and well until the moment I was telling what we found onboard Galahad at Bluff Cove. Unaccountably and very suddenly, when explaining about the young soldier we found welded to the deck, I burst into uncontrollable sobbing - something I swore I would never do and, indeed, had never done since the war. I had to turn away and it was several minutes before I was able to continue. Perhaps it takes thirty years and the intensity of filming to relive the events and to finally react to them.

Anyway, it affected me greatly and, shortly afterwards, I wrote the poem below.

10 January 2012

To a Young Galahad - Thirty Years on[1]

They brought their screens and smoke machines,
An HD camera and a Dolby mike
And, with a wooden bomb, a working fuze,
Selective lighting and some drapes,
Transformed my kitchen to a bombed-out ship
And said, "Tell us again what it was like."

I told them of the *Galahad,*
Of how we saved her that first, frightful night
When, from an acid-saturated wreck
That burned the clothing from our skin,
We worked to free a sleeping bomb and so

[1]See Bernie Bruen's earlier poem *To a Young Galahad. -* Sir Galahad was one of the Knights of the Round Table in the Arthurian legends. He was renowned for his bravery, kindness and purity. In the Falklands war one of the biggest disasters for the British side was the bombing of the supply ships *Sir Galahad* and *Sir Tristram.* Fifty-three men were killed and forty-six were seriously injured, many of them suffering horrific burns as the bombs had struck the ammunition store of the *Sir Galahad*, causing a huge fire which swept the ship.

Return her life, so nearly brought to waste.

I told them of the *Lancelot*,[1]
Of how we cut apart her gangways, worked
The night, and through the raids that terrorised
The day, to lift and shift and heave
And haul a dormant bomb from deep within
Until we could return her to the Fleet.
I told them, then, about Bluff Cove;

Of how we battled with the *Tristram*[2] blaze,
The four of us, to save her too - too late -
And blasted off her after door
So they could salvage shells and mortar-bombs,
Munitions for the hungry, Stanley guns.

And then again of *Galahad*
Who rocked and burned a pall of blackened flame
That rose from glowing bulkheads, blistered decks,
A signal column, dark above;
And you - for whom we could do nothing more
Than find a piece of canvas for a shroud.

Thirty years too late, unbidden,
Unexpected, unashamed, with sudden
Overflowing eyes, my message faltered;
For, though you never were forgot,
You're long past due those tears I shed for you;
As, in bewilderment, I turned away - and so did they.

Bernie Bruen

Kevin Abbott introduces his poem, Remember Still

At the time the Exocet missile struck the *Sheffield*, on 4 May 1982, I was
off watch and asleep. The missile struck the operations room and a fierce
fire soon raged, filling the ship with black, acrid, pungent smoke. There
were no pipes, broadcasts, or alarms. I joined in with the firefighting effort,

[1] *Sir Lancelot* was named after another of King Arthur's knights and also
involved in the Falklands war. It was struck by a bomb which did not explode.

[2] *Sir Tristram* was yet another knight of the round table and also, as just
mentioned, the name of a supply ship. It was bombed the same day as the *Sir
Galahad*.

spending time bailing free flood water between decks, running fore to aft with compressed air bottles, changing bottles etc. Later on, whilst ditching ammunition and avcat (aviation) fuel over the side, as the fires were still spreading, I learned that the rest of our entire watch had been overcome by smoke and had perished in the computer room trying to bring up the computers. These are the friends that I speak of in the poem. The *Sheffield* sank on the tenth of May.

Remember Still

I still can smell the heated steel
But the cold sea is all I feel
I still can taste the smoke and flame
Rising from where once laughter came
I still can hear the cries of men
Fighting the fear consuming them
I still can see those that still remain
As we abandoned this weary game

They are still, still there, still together
Still brothers in arms
At peace, all quiet, all still

I still smell the fog of that day in May
That covered up our aggressor's way
I still can see the confusion reign
In the eyes of those that try to explain
I still hear the sound of icy waves
Lapping the steel now their rusting grave
I still think back to that place in time
When luck ran out on friends of mine

They are still, still there, still together
Still brothers in arms
At peace, all quiet, all still
Still there

Kevin Abbott, *HMS Sheffield*

My Tribute

Words may be spun into threads, rich and fine,
To embroider in singular style
On the parchment of thought, where they gently entwine,
'Ere the page welcomes them with a smile.

These that I choose for this Tribute to you,
Have a poignant and powerful role,
Although simple, compared with work great poets do,
They've been spun in the depths of my soul.

From first invasion to Victory in June,
True support for the Falklands burned high,
Dockers toiled, knowing well they could lose their jobs soon,
All who sailed knew that many might die.

Mem'ries of aid so unselfishly given,
That aggression should win no acclaim,
Will bloom as a rose, with its roots set in Heaven,
Will burn like a perpetual flame.

Prayers were all heartfelt and truly sincere,
Grief was real when disaster occurred,
Like buds that unfold, springs that rise crystal clear,
Was your Country's great pride in you stirred.

Dear lads, sleeping now on land and at sea,
For your loved ones I pray with each thought,
Of you who've been injured I think constantly,
'Twas my Island home for which you fought.

God Bless you too with the scars that don't show,
May He guide and protect you wherever you go.

Lorena Triggs

About the Poets

Falkland Islands Writers

Ben Lovett is the history teacher at the secondary school in the Falkland Islands where he lives with his wife and two children (2012). His father, who was a medic with 3 Para, was killed in action on 12 June 1982 on Mount Longdon.

Lorena Triggs was born in the Falkland Islands in August 1939 and describes herself as "a proud Kelper". Her parents and grandparents were born on the islands, as was a maternal great, great-grandfather who was a Chelsea pensioner sent out to the Falklands in 1849. Her British-born husband went to the Falkland Islands in 1952. Lorena was married in 1957 and now has four children, eleven grandchildren and two great-grandchildren. She came to live in Britain in 1977, but with children living in the Falklands, she was following news of the Falklands War every inch of the way. She says that she wished that she had been there with them to know that they were safe.

British Writers

Kevin Abbott was born in Portsmouth in 1961. At the time of the Falklands war he was a weapon engineering apprentice on board *HMS Sheffield* when, on 4 May, it was hit by an Exocet missile fired from an Argentine Super-Etendard jet. The *Sheffield* had a crew of 280. Many of the twenty that died were friends of Kevin Abbott

Commander N A "Bernie" Bruen MBE DSC WKhM RN was born in Wales in 1946, brought up in Scotland and England, and now lives in France. His family is Irish. He is the son of World War II Fleet Air Arm fighter "Ace," Commander J M "Bill" Bruen DSO DSC RN. Although entering the Royal Navy as a helicopter pilot, Bernie soon transferred to the Diving Branch and, during the Falklands conflict, as a Lieutenant, commanded Fleet Clearance Diving Team Three, sixty-six percent of whom received gallantry awards. The team was the first to defuze an unknown enemy sea-mine by hand since the Korean War.

Eighteen months later, as Commanding Officer of *HMS Gavinton,* during the Red Sea mine clearance, he became the first to find an unknown enemy sea-mine by high definition sonar. For this he was made MBE.

He made a name for himself in Royal Navy boxing, mountaineering and rock climbing, as a ship-handler and sailor and as a poet, song writer, entertainer and fiddle player. He has three published books. Nowadays he keeps chickens.

> "We set a sail and see where it takes us.
> We make friends and then we move on.
> All we can do is to remember as best we can."   BB

Andrew Champion was born in Merton, then in Surrey now in Greater London, in October 1951. He served an engineering apprenticeship ashore before joining the merchant Navy. Ten years later the Falkland islands were invaded by Argentina. Andrew Champion was leaving a ship in Venice. He volunteered immediately for service on the *MV Anco Charger* as Third Engineer, a supply ship which had been taken up from trade by the Ministry of Defence. She was painted bright orange and carried, among other products, aviation fuel for the war in the Falklands.

Graham Cordwell was born in Cheltenham in April 1956. During the Falklands War he served as a Lieutenant Corporal in the Intelligence Section, HQ Company, Second Battalion, The Parachute Regiment.

The middle child of five, at the age of sixteen he joined the British Army. At the age of eighteen he was posted to Second Battalion of The Parachute Regiment (2 Para) with whom he served for nearly fifteen years before resigning in March 1988.

During his time in the army he served four tours of duty in Northern Ireland and saw active service in the Falklands War in 1982. He married in 1978 and has two children. Unfortunately the marriage didn't survive the Falklands War and he divorced in 1986. He served as a police officer for three years in the Surrey Constabulary, England, before resigning and moving to Norway with his new wife in 1991.

In 1994 at the age of thirty-eight he went to college to train as a social worker and thereafter worked with people with drug and alcohol problems. In 2002, after a mental breakdown, he was diagnosed with chronic PTSD. He then spent five years in treatment and rehabilitation. He writes, "I am eternally grateful to my wife who manages to keeps me sane. I hope to be well again one day."

Graham Cordwell shares a belief with Tony McNally that the British army has not done enough to look after the many veterans who develop serious psychological problems as a result of their war experiences.

Cesca M Croft (not her real name) was born in London in 1947.

Gus Hales served as a paratrooper in the Falklands War. Subsequently he suffered from post traumatic stress disorder. Gus revisited the Falklands in 2007 when, on Remembrance Day, at a service in Christ Church Cathedral in Stanley, feeling the voice of the ordinary soldier was rarely heard, he stood up, walked to the front of the cathedral and addressed the distinguished congregation. His contribution was not scheduled. He then recited his poem. We have transcribed the poem from a recording of a Falkland Islands Radio broadcast and given it a title which we hope Gus would approve of, *Victory*.

James Love was born in Glasgow in 1955. He trained as a paratrooper and served in Germany, the Falklands and the French Foreign Legion. This is his story.

I joined the army after a brief spell in the City of Glasgow Police. I volunteered for Parachute training in February of 1974. After passing P Company and completing my jump training, I joined "I" Parachute Battery, Bull's Troop, 7th Parachute Regiment, Royal Horse Artillery. In 1979 I disappeared whilst in the BAOR (British Army of the Rhine), Germany and joined the French Foreign Legion where I made the rank of Corporal. Unfortunately, the pay and conditions were not the greatest and I decided to "leave" and rejoin the British Army. After getting out of France, I hitch-hiked back to Osnabruck in West Germany where my unit was now stationed - walking the last eighty kilometres in a blizzard.

After being tried by Court-Martial (under Section 38 of the Army Act 1955) I served seven months and eleven days in prison (six weeks of it in solitary) having earned three months and four days remission of sentence for good behaviour. I returned to Aldershot and joined the Parachute contingent of

4th Field Regiment Royal Artillery and was attached initially to B Company of the 2nd Battalion the Parachute Regiment as a member of the Forward Observation Party (as a signaller directing artillery fire).

I was then transferred to A Company whilst on top of Sussex Mountains in the Falkland Islands in May 1982. I served on attachment to A Company until June 1982 when we returned to the Battery (29 Corunna 4th Field Regiment, Royal Artillery) and 2 Para sailed home to the UK on the *Norland*. We flew out some weeks later after being roped in to guard the prisoners on the *St Edmund* ferry.

I bought myself out of the Army in 1991 for £200 and am now employed by the Ministry of Defence Police Guarding Agency working at the Royal School of Artillery in Wiltshire. JL

Lisa Lutwyche was born in February 1955 in Bethesda, Maryland, USA. She has been a published poet for several decades. She also spent 28 years in the practice of corporate and institutional architecture and design.

During intense surgical and chemical treatments for breast cancer, she was fired from her job in architecture and spent her life savings to complete the cancer treatments. (She says, "Never complain about your National Health Service.") Lisa is now a part-time optician (so she can have health care), a writer, art instructor, and playwright, teaching writing and art in four venues, including a community college. She is halfway through a Master of Fine Arts degree in Creative Writing (2012). She lives with her British-born husband, Nicholas, in a small house in the Pennsylvania forest with their seven rescued cats.

Nicholas Lutwyche was born in 1943 in Barton-on-Sea, Hampshire, UK. He joined the Royal Navy at the age of 18 and qualified as an aircraft mechanic. He joined *HMS Invincible* in 1981 as an engineering Fleet Chief Petty Officer. In April 1982 he was on a week's leave at home in Milton Abbas, Dorset when he received an early morning phone call summoning him back to Portsmouth as the ship was preparing to sail for the Falkland Islands at very short notice. He returned home on 17 September 1982.

Lt Mark Mathewson, Right Flank 2nd Battalion Scots Guards served in the Falklands War.

Tony McNally was born in July 1962 in Barrow-in-Furness. He joined the Army at the age of 16 and survived the harsh training (which he vividly describes in his book, *Watching Men Burn - a Soldier's Story*) to go on to train as a gunner operating a Rapier missile launcher. When he was 19 he was sent to the Falklands. At a crucial moment, when an Argentine Sky Hawk jet roared towards him to bomb the *Sir Galahad*, the launcher jammed and the *Sir Galahad* went up in flames. This event has haunted Tony McNally ever since. He went on to serve in Northern Ireland but found his war experience had changed him completely. Nightmares and hallucinations, started to seriously affect his life. His marriage was suffering and his wife feared actual harm. He sought help and was eventually diagnosed by a civilian doctor as suffering from post traumatic stress disorder, a condition the British army refused to accept existed. He vividly describes the condition in his poetry and in his book. He is aware that his writing has helped others to acknowledge their difficulties, get help and save their lives.

Louise Russell (not her real name) was born in Londonderry, Northern Ireland in 1951.

Argentine Writers

José Luis Aparicio is an Argentine born in the vicinity of Treinta de Agosto in October 1961. As a conscript he fought in the Falklands War. He belongs to the activist organization CECIM, Centre of Ex-combatants of the Malvinas Islands.

Maria Cristina Azcona was born in Buenos Aires. She works as an educational psychologist, family counsellor and specialist in forensic psycho-diagnosis. She is a bilingual poet, writer and editor with six published books: four in Argentina and two in India, in English and Spanish. She has written approximately a thousand critical articles and poems, published worldwide in newspapers, anthologies, magazines, e-zines and poetry books.

She has coauthored *Peace, Literature and Art*, for an e-book edited by UNESCO and coauthored another e-book for the Unesco EOLSS Encyclopaedia. Books published in Argentina: *Dos Talles Menos de Cerebro, Mundo Postmoderno, La Voz del Ángel, Estar de Novios Hoy (junto a Ernesto Castellano, su esposo)*.

Juan Carlos Escalante is an Argentine poet, novelist, critic and journalist. He was born in March 1945.

Luz Etchemendigaray is Argentine, born in the Province of Entre Rios. She is a novelist and poet and has published numerous books.

Julia Garzón-Fuentes is an Argentine poet.

Daniel Ginhson is an Argentine poet, cineaste and translator. He was born in 1932.

Ange Kenny is a poet born in Buenos Aires.

Sue Littleton is a poet born in Abilene, Texas, September 1932. Her poems have been published in various anthologies and literary magazines. Her most important book is the bilingual epic poem *Corn Woman, Mujer Maíz*. She is one of the four founders of the Austin (Texas) International Poetry Festival.

She married an Argentine lawyer studying International Law at university in 1957. Her husband's brother was Minister of Mining under President Illia and her husband was a political writer as well as a corporate lawyer. Three children were born to the marriage, which lasted 13 years. Sue remained in Buenos Aires four more years; the last four years during the tumultuous '70s. She published her first book of poetry, in Spanish, *Imágenes* in 1972. She attended psychology classes and there met young Argentine liberal poets who introduced her to members of Leftist political groups. At the same time she maintained contact with the more conservative middle class.

When people began to disappear, were being arrested, kidnapped, and taken away to be tortured and murdered, Sue was directly involved in several incidents to protect persons persecuted by the regime. In November 1976 she was becoming aware that being an American citizen was not a guarantee against official aggression if she continued her political and literary agenda. She returned to Texas but later made annual visits to Argentina.

Sue always said that although she and her Argentine husband were divorced, she never divorced Argentina, and that one day she would return to live out the rest of her days in her adopted country. She has eight (surviving) Argentine grandchildren. She moved permanently to Buenos Aires in 2005.

Alfredo María Villegas Oromí is an Argentine poet who was born in April 1955 and is an agronomist now living in Uruguay.

Martín Raninqueo was born in La Plata, Argentina, in 1962. Musician and poet, ex-combatant of the Malvinas. His latest book is an illustrated book of haiku, *Haikus of War* (of the Malvinas). Martín is a descendant of a cacique (a Native American leader, or chief, of a tribe local to Argentina) Borogano Andrers Raninqueo, who lived in Laguna La Verde (Green Lake), Province of Buenos Aires. Martín was a soldier conscript in the 7th Infantry Regiment Coronel Conde; he was in his first year of university when he was summarily drafted and sent to the Malvinas. He fought in the Section of the Heavy Mortars in Mount Wireless Ridge. He was captured as a prisoner of war and returned to Argentina in the English ship, *HMS Canberra*.

Roberto Ronquietto is an Argentine poet born in the Province of San Juan.

Adriana Scalese is a psychologist, teacher and poet. She was born in September 1957.

Maria Graciela Romero Sosa is Argentine, born in Buenos Aires in November 1955. She is the author of stories and poems which have been widely published. She is a psychologist.

Nina Thürler is a well-known Argentine poet, born August 1942 in Buenos Aires and the author of fourteen books.

.

Unusual expressions

Binos - binoculars

Bluie - a "letter-form" that is issued to service personnel for "letters home".

Cammy- camouflage

Cowboy - An expression commonly used in Britain with derogatory connotations. It is applied to tradesmen who have little or no professional training, lack knowledge and skills, give confident assurances of their abilities, charge high prices and do incompetent or even disastrous work.

Dhobi - washing, laundry.

Fuze - alternative spelling of "fuse".

Helo - soldier's slang for helicopter.

HMS - Her Majesty's Ship.

Las Malvinas or Islas Malvinas - the name used by the Argentines for The Falkland Islands.

Peronist - supporter of Juan Domingo Perón, three times President of Argentina or someone who espouses his left wing ideas.

Picana - electric cattle prod.

PTSD - Post Traumatic Stress Disorder. A serious, debilitating mental condition brought on by high levels of stress such as those experienced by soldiers who have engaged in fighting. It affects personal relationships and ability to cope with everyday life. It is treatable, especially if diagnosed early.

Red white and blue - the British flag.

RFA - Royal Fleet Auxiliary. Ships owned by the British Ministry of Defence and manned by civilians.

Rovers - Landrover 4x4 vehicles.

Sangar - a sort of wall built with stones or sods of earth or peat to make a protective barrier behind which soldiers might find protection.

SAS - Special Air Service. An elite corps of the British army.

SBS - Special Boat Service. An elite corps of the British Navy.

Soledad Island - East Falkland Island. Soledad was the name used by the Spanish and Argentines. It means "solitude".

UXB - unexploded bomb.

David Roberts

David Roberts, the editor of this book, was born in Spalding, Lincolnshire, UK, in October 1942. He is a writer and publisher, and the editor of the war poetry website: www.warpoetry.co.uk .

His books include:

Two very successful anthologies of poetry of the First World War: *Out in the dark, Poetry of the First World War, in context and with basic notes*, and *Minds at War, The Poetry and Experience of the First World War.*

Kosovo War Poetry (ISBN 0 952 8969 2 3) about the war in Kosovo in 1999 and the NATO bombing campaign.

The European Union and You, a guide to the European Union, its origins, development, problems and potential.

Lessons from Iraq, the UN must be reformed. Published by Action for UN Renewal. (A pamphlet.)

The European Union and You
By David Roberts

This is a highly readable account of the European Union written for the ordinary citizen and students. It explores the ideas which guide it, its institutions, its policies, its successes, and its failings. This book is both a detailed reference book and a critical assessment. Published at the end of 2007 it contains the text of the EU Constitution. This with small modifications became the Lisbon Treaty which currently governs the workings of the EU and is therefore still of interest.

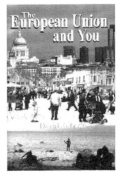

Although much has changed since this book was written and sections are, therefore, out of date, it remains an invaluable and clear guide to Europe's most powerful and least understood political institution. The few remaining copies may possibly be bought at a bargain price.

620 pages. Hardback. ISBN 978-0-9528969-4-4
Published by Saxon Books

Also published by Saxon Books

Out in the Dark
Poetry of the First World War
In context and with basic notes
Edited by David Roberts

This 192 page anthology contains the most important poems and poets of the First World War, but there are also many other poets of special interest, with women poets particularly well represented. The most celebrated poets - including Wilfred Owen, Siegfried Sassoon and Isaac Rosenberg - have been given whole chapters. Their work has been arranged in date order so that the development of their ideas and techniques may be appreciated.

Comments of past and present day critics, and basic explanatory notes on unusual expressions and vocabulary make this poignant anthology especially valuable for students. Extracts from poets' diaries and letters, historical and biographical notes, plus fascinating photographs and drawings give further insights into the experience and thinking of the war poets.

Eighth printing. 192 pages 9"x6" Paperback Illustrated
ISBN 978-0-9528969-1-3
£8-99

Minds at War
The Poetry and Experience of the First World War
Edited by David Roberts

The Classic poems (Wilfred Owen, Siegfried Sassoon, Isaac Rosenberg, and others), plus women poets and popular verse - in all, 250 poems by 80 poets. This encyclopaedic volume also includes extracts from poets' letters and diaries, pronouncements by the media, leading commentators and politicians of the day, historic photographs and cartoons, maps biographies and historical background material.

410 pages. Paperback. Illustrated.
Seventh printing. ISBN 978-0-952 8969-0-6
£14-99 UK